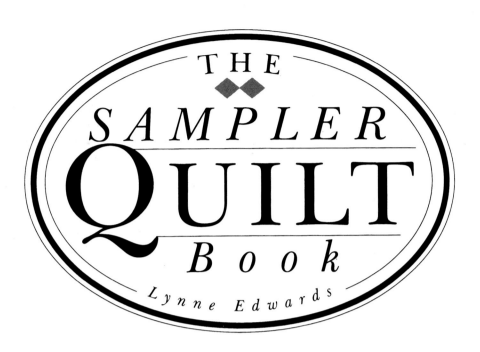

THE
SAMPLER
QUILT
Book

Lynne Edwards

To

Meryl —

All best wishes,

Lynne Edwards

May 2001

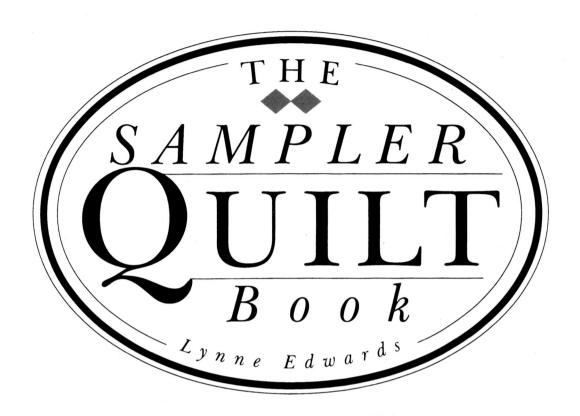

THE
SAMPLER
QUILT
Book

Lynne Edwards

David & Charles

To the ever supportive Brian, Dickon and Tom,
Mum and Dad.
To Wendy Crease and Pepper Cory, dear friends
whose help and encouragement has opened so
many exciting doors.
Finally, to all those nervous, anxious-to-please,
first-time quilters who signed on and turned up
to make a sampler quilt. My local classes are my
bread and butter. They are also the jam and the
icing on the cake. Heartfelt thanks.

Lynne

A DAVID & CHARLES BOOK

First published in the UK in 1996
Reprinted in 1997, 1998, 2000
Text and designs Copyright © Lynne Edwards 1996
Photography and layout Copyright © David & Charles 1996

Lynne Edwards has asserted her right to be identified as author of this
work in accordance with the Copyright, Designs and Patents Act, 1988.

A catalogue record for this book is available from the British Library.

ISBN 0 7153-0311-2

Photography by Alan Duns and Paul Biddle
Book design by Maggie Aldred
Typeset by Greenshires Icon, Exeter
and printed in Italy by Lego SpA
for David & Charles
Brunel House Newton Abbot Devon

CONTENTS

INTRODUCTION

A sampler quilt is one of the best ways to get started on patchwork and quilting. It enables you to try a variety of sewing and design techniques and see how you like them. Whilst some will become favourites, others will be put into the 'never again' category. It also allows you to experiment with colour, combining plain fabrics with prints or textures. Although everyone finds this particular skill daunting at first, it does get easier the more often you do it. But, best of all, you get to make a real quilt from start to finish, joining the quilted squares, dealing with borders and quilt edgings and then finally stitching your name and the date on to the completed heirloom.

For some years I have run a one-year course on making a sampler quilt. It comprises five full-day sessions over each of three terms, with the students learning two techniques at each session: one based on handwork, the other using a quick machine method. Usually the hand-sewn design is begun in class and then taken away, hopefully to be finished during the intervening two weeks. The machine-stitched design is often completed during the session.

After the first three or four sessions I teach hand-quilting, so that the squares, known as blocks, can be quilted individually before joining them together at the finish. This 'quilt as you go' approach is not favoured by some other experienced quilters, but I believe it to be preferable to joining all the completed blocks together at the end of the course and then sending everyone on their way to try and quilt it for themselves. The size of the project would be too daunting for first-time quilters and many would never finish.

By the third term, all the different techniques have been taught and the students have made at least twenty blocks. They now learn how to join the blocks together, how to design and make the borders and how to finish off. I *have* had students whose diligence and commitment have been exemplary and who have kept up with every stage, quilting away during the Christmas break, completing squares over Easter and bringing their quilt ready for signing on the last festive session. I have also known some equally enthusiastic quilters who have taken a full two years to finish, as families, careers and life in general have got in the way. None of this matters: the object of the exercise is just to enjoy.

This book has been devised from the course and can be used in several ways. You can start at the first technique and work through each block, just as if you were attending my course. (The order of the blocks has been carefully sequenced so that the skills learned from one technique are used and built upon in the next.) Alternatively you can use the book as an encyclopaedia of techniques. You can select individual patterns and try them out, using the instructions given for that block to make a single 12in (30.5cm) finished sample which can then be developed into a project like a cushion, bag or small wallhanging. Or you could make a quilt using just one repeated block, or a combination of two or three blocks arranged and repeated in the way you like best.

The section at the end of the book takes some of the techniques and expands them into a variety of projects of all sizes. I hope this particular section will help and inspire quilters to use their favourite designs from the sampler quilt and develop them into projects of their own in the future.

Remember – only make a quilt for someone if you know they are aching to possess it. Make it for yourself because you want to. Keep it yourself and enjoy it until the right person comes along and falls in love with it. Then you know you have found the right owner and you will all live happily ever after.

Opposite Lynne Edwards, *pictured top right, runs a popular course on making a sampler quilt.*

GETTING STARTED

So you are thinking about making a
sampler quilt? No doubt you have a long
list of questions you would like answered
before you can even start thinking
about putting needle to fabric.
To get you going, here are some of the
facts you need to know about choosing
and preparing the materials.

How Much Fabric Do I Need?

For a single bed quilt you need about 6yd (5.5m) of
45in (115cm) wide fabric for the front of the quilt.
For a double bed quilt you need about 9yd (8.25m)
for the quilt top. Although it seems logical to plan all
the fabrics required for the quilt first and buy them
all at once, selecting one fabric for the strips that
frame each block and another for the border etc,
experience has shown me that it is better to wait
until several blocks have been made and the overall
balance of colour is developing before choosing the
fabric, or fabrics, to frame the blocks. Choosing border fabrics really does need to be left until the blocks
are joined, as only then can you lay other fabrics
alongside the work to see which effect looks best.
This does seem like living dangerously – what if they
haven't got any more of that fabric left? What if you
don't have enough? When that happens you just
have to choose something else, which will make the
quilt richer and more adventurous.

Initially work with about six fabrics, possibly half
patterned and half plain; 20in (50cm) of each will be
sufficient. As the quilt grows you will need more, but
it is easier to choose when you have some completed
blocks to refer to. If it is not possible to buy some
more of one of your chosen fabrics, find another similar in colour, you can get a great deal of pleasure
adding to your palette of fabrics as you go along.
Specialist quilt shops stock a huge selection of fabrics
manufactured especially for patchwork and many
operate a mail order service.

With the 'quilt as you go' technique, both batting,
the layer between the front and back of the quilt,
and backing fabric are cut into 15in (38cm) squares
rather than used in one large piece, so any width is
suitable. As a guide, you need 6yd (5.5m) of 45in
(115cm) wide batting and backing fabric for a single

bed quilt. You may have to do some calculations to
find the equivalent amount if either batting or backing fabric is much wider than this. When in doubt,
always buy too much if you can afford to, any excess
can always be used in future projects. If you are on
a very limited budget there is nothing to stop you
using a variety of fabrics for the backing squares.
That way you get a patchwork effect on both sides!

What Sort Of Fabric Can I Use?

The traditional image of a patchwork quilt is that of
an economy craft, patching and piecing with any
scraps available. This can still hold true today, but it
is as well to know what fabrics to avoid and what to
choose to make the cutting and stitching easier and
more enjoyable and to ensure that the completed
quilt becomes a long-lasting heirloom.

Most dressmaking scraps are made of synthetic
materials, like polyester and viscose. Unfortunately
these do not combine with other fabrics very successfully, unless the project is a marvellously
textured, contemporary wallhanging where durabil-
ity is not a consideration. If you want to make a
patchwork quilt which will last for years, mellowing
and becoming even more beautiful as it ages, then
use a combination of pure cotton fabrics. The thickness of these fabrics needs to be consistent: a
medium-weight cotton is easier to work with than
lightweight lawns; heavier soft-furnishing fabrics are
fine for machined quilts which use large pieces, but
would not be suitable for this sampler.

Look for fabrics which provide a good balance of
plains, large and small designs, and light, medium
and dark tones. This may seem impossible when you
begin but it gets easier as the work progresses, so
limiting your initial selection of fabrics helps.

I'm No Use At Choosing Colours

This is a familiar cry. It should really be replaced
with, 'I'm not experienced in choosing colours so
that the mixture has balance'. Colour itself is very
personal – it is also strongly influenced by fashion.
As a young girl I learned that 'blue and green should
never be seen', I also remember the shock of seeing
pink and orange together in the Sixties. But fashion
moves on and the unacceptable becomes comfortable, even the names change so that fawn and beige

have become ecru and taupe. Soft-furnishing design plays its part too. The first quilt you make is usually for a planned position, it has to go in a certain room and tone with the carpet and wallpaper. It must coordinate rather than make its own loud statement, so soft, restful shades are most favoured. Sunshine and quality of light will also influence your choice.

In low-lying East Anglia, where I have my home, there is a lot of sky which is more often grey-blue than blue, as is the sea. I like to work in subtle shades of cool colours which I'm sure is dictated by the quality of the light. Warmer countries with fierce sunshine, a deep blue sky and vivid landscapes demand stronger colours. My silvers, greys and blues would look very out of place in Australia and if I lived there it would not be long I'm sure before I began working with a palette of clear, vibrant colours. Add to these external influences your own personal preferences and you can see the impossibility of dictating what you must or must not choose.

Start by selecting a fabric that you really like. Never mind if everyone else thinks it is dull or sweetly-pretty, brash or downright ugly. If it jumps off the shelf at you crying 'Take me, I'm yours', then start with that fabric. If you want your quilt to be essentially just one colour then make sure there is plenty of variation in the shades you use. You will need some light or pale shades as well as some dark or stronger ones. Place your chosen fabrics together and look at them through half-closed eyes. If it is difficult to see where one fabric ends and another begins you will need to introduce some that give definition to your selection. Without this your quilt could look very bland, as if it had been printed overall rather than assembled from different fabrics.

If you want a real contrast of colours, like a red and white quilt, add textures, spots, checks and small and large prints to the basic plain red and white scheme. Do not coordinate too desperately, or it will resemble the printed patchwork look. Introduce something surprising, an element only you could have thought of; a large print which uses red and white plus black might just give that extra accent or zing to the quilt.

Seek advice from a like-minded enthusiast or from someone whose colour sense you admire; you will never be imposing on the time of a true fabric addict. Do not bother with the rest of your family, though, if they do not share your enthusiasm and they sigh and shift from foot to foot after five minutes in a quilt shop. Finally, when everyone has offered their opinion, remember that it is your quilt and it has to please *you*. The limited selection of fabrics that you start with will grow along with your confidence as work on the blocks progresses.

What About The Batting?

Between the front and back of the quilt is the layer known as wadding, which gives the padded effect. It is also known as batting, which is the American terminology and brand names will call it batting, as do most of the European quilters, and so, therefore, have I. Suppliers offer a wide range of different battings, some polyester, some cotton and some even pure silk, but save your experimenting for small projects, as once you start on your sampler quilt you need to use the same batting throughout.

Polyester batting is available in two to six and even eight ounce weights, although the thicker battings are more suitable for tied quilts and not for a hand-quilted project like this. For your sampler quilt I would recommend a two ounce polyester batting, known in the United States as Low-Loft. Because the blocks are quilted individually you do not need to buy a large piece of batting. You may change your mind about the final size of your quilt, so make sure your batting comes from a reliable supplier who will always have that particular one in stock.

How Do I Prepare The Fabrics?

It has always been impressed upon me that all fabrics must be washed before they are used for patchwork and it is always the safest thing to do. However, if, like me, you enjoy working with fresh, crisp, unwashed fabric, you must at least test any strong or dark colours for colourfastness before you begin. Wash these separately, using soap flakes or a gentle, non-biological liquid, and check that the colour does not leak out into the water. You just cannot take risks with colours like red, indigo, wine etc, and I have got several disaster stories to prove it. As for shrinkage, I do not worry about this when I am using special patchwork fabrics, but I certainly do not trust furnishing cottons or fashion fabrics and always wash them before use. Try to iron the fabrics whilst they are still slightly damp to ensure a smooth finish.

It may be stating the obvious, but batting does not usually need pre-washing (unless it is one of the newer cotton varieties, which come with appropriate instructions) and it certainly does not need ironing. *Never* put an iron directly on to polyester batting as it melts instantly. You should only iron batting that is sandwiched between layers of fabric, but beware of using steam or a hot iron, as the batting can bond on to the fabric and give an unattractive stiff feeling. Only press batting if you really have to, and then only use a cool, dry iron and there should be no problem.

BASIC EQUIPMENT

There is an increasingly wide range of tools and gadgets available, from specialist shops and quilt shows, designed especially for quilters. On many occasions students have shown me a special ruler or odd-shaped piece of plastic and said: 'I know this is really useful, but I can't remember why...' If you are a beginner and the sampler quilt is your first major project, stick to the basic equipment listed in this section. Once you are totally hooked and you have the next three quilt projects planned, then you will find all sorts of wonderful aids to accuracy and techniques that you cannot live without.

For Hand-sewing

Needles: Personally I really dislike packets of assorted needles as they usually contain only two sizes that you can use – the rest will come in useful for stitching up the turkey at Christmas! Try to buy packets of one size only if possible as it is more economical. Also if you lose needles as often as I do you will need a whole packet about your person. Sharps size 9 or 10 are best for piecing and appliqué, while Betweens size 9 or 10 are best for quilting.

Pins: There are many types of pins on the market and each one has a different function. I like to use long, fine dressmaker's pins (called extra-fine, extra-long), although other people favour the coloured, glass-headed type as they are easier to hold and to find when dropped on the carpet. Buy the smaller, fine variety rather than the huge quilt pins, these should only be used to pin thick, layered quilts together and are just too big for normal pinning. You can buy plastic-headed pins, but do remember that the plastic heads will melt under a hot iron. If you use these pins this is not a problem, just take care when you are pressing. Another type available is a tiny pin used for appliqué, which is useful for holding small pieces in position. These pins are known as Lills as well as appliqué pins. You do not need all the types of pins described; one will do as long as they are fine and you are comfortable using them.

Thimble: I was never taught to sew with a thimble. Come to think of it, I was never taught to sew... For years I stitched without a thimble, but then found I needed one for quilting and now I cannot work without one. Wear a thimble for handwork if you like, but do not feel you absolutely *have* to. However, a thimble really is needed for quilting, to protect the middle finger of your dominant hand. A flat-topped thimble is the best shape for quilting.

Thread: For sewing cotton fabrics I like to use a good quality, pure cotton thread, although cotton-coated polyester is a good alternative. Try to match the colour of the thread as closely as possible to the fabrics. If using a mixture of colours, go for a darker rather than a lighter shade. The best test for colour match is to lay a thread across the fabric to see if it virtually disappears.

For quilting, pure cotton quilting thread is ideal. It is stronger, thicker and waxed to give a smooth thread that tangles less than ordinary sewing thread.

Scissors: You will need a sharp, medium-sized pair of scissors for cutting the fabric, plus a larger pair purely for paper cutting. A pair of small, really sharp scissors with good points will be useful for clipping seams and trimming thread.

Fabric Markers: A quilt should last decades, so you need to think of its future. Although you need some sort of fabric marker to mark template shapes on to the fabric and indicate quilting lines, beware of the spirit pens that are available, even if they are water erasable. They are excellent for dressmaking, but make a harsh line and, as yet, it is not known whether the chemicals used in them will eventually rot the fabric. Specialist quilt shops sell silver, white and yellow marking pencils which can be sharpened to a fine point for accuracy. Read the packaging carefully before you use them; if it says 'will not fade' it is fine for marking around templates but not suitable for quilting.

Always test the marker on a spare piece of fabric before you start work and check that it can be erased. You can buy a fabric eraser suitable for use with these markers.

For quilting I use Aquarelle coloured pencils in the softest quality available; they can be bought from art shops. Choose a shade similar to the fabric but dark enough to be seen clearly. The line wears off

Basic equipment should include a selection of different needles, pins and threads. More specialist quilting equipment is an option rather than an essential.

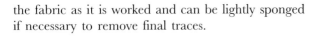

the fabric as it is worked and can be lightly sponged if necessary to remove final traces.

Tape Measure: Extra long tape measures can now be bought, and are 100in (2.5m) or longer with metric markings on the reverse. They are particularly useful for the longer measurements that have to be made when you are making up a quilt. Remember your grandmother's ancient linen tape could have stretched and may not be accurate.

Quilter's Quarter and Seamwheel: These two tools are used to draw an accurate $\frac{1}{4}$in (6mm) cutting line beyond the template outline. The quarter is placed against the marked line and drawn along the outer edge. The seamwheel is rolled round the edge of the template itself by a pencil point which is fixed in the centre hole. As the wheel moves round, the pencil marks a line $\frac{1}{4}$in (6mm) from the template edge. Personally I do not bother with either of these but just cut the seam allowances by eye. However, many quilters do find them very useful, so try them for yourself and find out.

Bias-Maker and Bias Bars: The Bias-Maker is a dressmaking tool which turns cut bias strips into the familiar folded strip of fabric seen in commercial bias binding. In the sampler quilt it is used to create the strips for the leaded effect in Stained Glass patchwork. The width of bias-makers ranges from $\frac{1}{2}$in (1.2cm) to 2in (5cm), but the $\frac{1}{2}$in (1.2cm) is most suitable for Stained Glass patchwork. Bias Bars are another useful tool, this time produced specifically for quilters to make Celtic patchwork, where narrow strips of fabric are appliquéd on to a background in traditional Celtic interlaced patterns. There are several widths of bar from the narrowest at $\frac{1}{8}$in (3mm) to $\frac{1}{2}$in (1.2cm). The $\frac{1}{4}$in (6mm) width is most suitable for Stained Glass in the sampler quilt.

Masking Tape: Special $\frac{1}{4}$in (6mm) masking tape is sold in quilt shops and is really useful for marking the straight lines for quilting. Avoid the wider varieties sold in stationers and do-it-yourself shops as they are not the low-tack variety which you need for sticking on to fabric. Even when using the $\frac{1}{4}$in (6mm) tape, do not leave it on the fabric any longer than necessary just in case it leaves a mark.

For Making The Templates

Many of the block designs need templates which have to be copied from instructions and transferred on to card or template plastic. Accuracy is critical here so you will need very sharp pencils, a good pencil sharpener, eraser, ruler, tracing paper and card or template plastic.

Template plastic is widely available from specialist quilt shops and other outlets selling sewing equipment. It makes a good alternative to card as templates made from it can be saved and used over and over again. The plastic is clear and firm, yet pliable and easy to cut with scissors, and it is available in two types: a plain, clear variety and one which is marked with a measured grid. Both are usually sold in packs of A4 and A3 size sheets.

You also need a water-soluble glue stick and a 12in (30.5cm) ruler.

Graph paper is very useful for drafting your own patterns and borders. It is not easy to find paper with Imperial measurements as the major stationery stores stock metric only, but quilt shops often have A4 pads marked in $\frac{1}{4}$in (6mm) squares. Quality art shops usually stock large sheets of graph paper marked in inches, but beware of buying any with $\frac{1}{10}$in (2.5mm) markings, as they do not show the $\frac{1}{4}$in (6mm) divisions and if you find anything other than simple sums difficult it could present a problem.

Freezer Paper: Freezer paper is becoming very popular for appliqué work in the USA. It looks like greaseproof paper but is slightly thicker and has a shiny side which sticks to the fabric when it is ironed. This makes it particularly useful for appliqué work because it keeps small shapes firm as they are stitched in place. After use the paper can be peeled off the fabric, without leaving any marks, and reused. Currently freezer paper is only available from specialist quilt shops.

A good substitute is the thick paper used to wrap large packs of photocopying paper. If you know anyone who works in an office, ask them to pass some on.

For Machine Work

Sewing Machine: This does not have to be a state of the art model. It just needs to be one you enjoy using and reliable, a machine that will not suddenly have hysterics and munch up your fabric. If you have had your machine for years and never changed the needle or oiled it, this could be classed as criminal neglect. Treat the poor thing to a service or at least a new needle and a thorough clean and some oil before you embark on your sampler quilt.

Use a size 11/80 needle for medium-weight cotton fabrics and remember that it should be changed after at least every eight sewing hours. You soon clock up the hours with machine patchwork, so buy a packet of needles and *use* them.

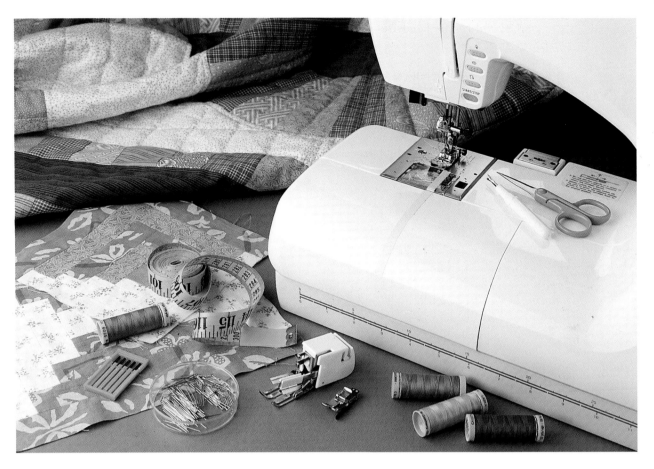

A straight-stitch foot is ideal for machine patch-work. You need to stitch straight seams that are exactly ¼in (6mm) from the needle, so a narrow straight-stitch foot is very helpful. So too is the ¼in (6mm) foot that some sewing machine manufacturers have produced especially for quilters. A walking foot is useful for stitching through layers of fabric and batting, as it prevents the top fabric from creeping ahead of the other layers and giving a twisted effect. It also makes sewing on the final binding to the quilt much easier and is essential if you venture into machine quilting.

Thread: Use the same cotton or cotton-coated polyester thread as for hand-sewing. A sewing machine is colour blind and is quite happy to have one shade as the top thread and another on the bobbin; what it does hate is mixing different brands of thread as they do not have the same density as each other. Choose one manufacturer and stick to their thread throughout.

Stitch Ripper: An invaluable little tool, although I seldom use it for unpicking stitches. I do use it as an extra finger to hold fabric in place while feeding it under the machine foot. The point sticks into the

A well-maintained sewing machine is an essential for machine work on the sampler quilt. New needles and a good quality thread will help to get good results.

fabric slightly and keeps the layers in place right up to the needle without any danger. It can also prevent the seam allowances from being pushed in the wrong direction by the machine foot as you sew.

Pins: For any machine work I prefer the extra-fine, extra-long pins as they slip out of the fabric so easily. However, if glass- or plastic-headed pins are your favourites, and you can use them efficiently, then do so.

For Rotary Cutting

Once you start using a rotary cutter, ruler and mat, you will wonder how you ever managed without them. These three items are expensive, so you may want to borrow them for a while from a fellow quilter until you have mastered their use. However, you will soon find that you cannot get on without them and have to invest in your own set.

There are several different mats on the market, but do get one with an inch grid marked on it. The

◆◆

back is usually plain, which makes it a useful surface for arranging designs, as it is also non-slip. There are several sizes of mat, but the most useful for patchwork is the 23 x 17in (58.5 x 43cm). If you try to economize and buy the smaller size you will soon regret it. The really big mat is ideal if you have a permanent work surface at home, but is very awkward to take out to classes as it must not be rolled. Whatever you do, do not leave your mat in the back of the car in summer or against a radiator in winter; it will warp and nothing you do will return it to its original flat state. Always follow what it says in the instructions printed on the mat itself: store flat out of direct sunlight.

The mat is also self-healing when a rotary cutter is used on it and the cutting marks disappear, providing you use the appropriate cutter. Craft knives and other blades do real damage, so do not let the family model-maker near it.

Cutters vary in design and more are appearing on the market; see what other quilters or shop owners recommend, try them and use whichever one you like best. I still like the cutter that I started with, which is what many of us seem to do. Cutters come in two sizes, so if you feel nervous it is a good idea to start with the small one, which does not seem so lethal. The small cutter can cut through up to four layers of fabric efficiently and is always the best one to use when cutting round small shapes, especially curved edges. I own both large and small cutters which I use for different tasks – I also have mega-large cutters which cut sixteen layers or more, but that seems a little like boasting, so I won't mention them again.

The blades do get blunt with use and must be replaced at intervals. If your blade is leaving tiny fibres of thread trapped in the cut surface of the mat, you need a new one. Often it is only when you use someone else's cutter that you realize just how blunt your own has become. If you are unlucky enough to run over a pin when cutting, the cutting edge will be damaged and you will need a new blade. The large cutter is more obviously lethal and you need to develop the habit of always pushing the guard back into place directly you have finished using it. The assembly nut should be loosened off when it is in use and then tightened up again for storage. Occasionally the whole thing should be dismantled and cleaned with a smidgen of oil on a soft cloth.

Special rulers have to be used with the mat and cutter. This is not just a marketing ploy because the cutter will shave off the edges of wooden and metal rulers and even the ordinary, school plastic rulers. Rotary rulers are about $\frac{1}{8}$in (3m) thick and are made of tough perspex. There are dozens of different types on sale: some non-slip, some with black, yellow or white markings, some narrow and some wide. Choose one with markings that you feel comfortable reading and which measures up to 24in (61cm). This size will work well on your folded fabric and on the medium-sized cutting mat. You can buy a $12\frac{1}{2}$in (31.7cm) square perspex ruler which would be a wonderful addition to your equipment if you can afford it, as each block for the sampler quilt has to measure exactly $12\frac{1}{2}$in (31.7cm) square before the framing sashing strips are added. However, it is purely a luxury item and not essential.

Quilters often find it difficult to cut small pieces of fabric freehand using a rotary cutter. There is an attachment called a guide arm that you can fix on to either large or small cutters to help you. It can be adjusted so that the black arm is $\frac{1}{4}$in (6mm) from the blade and, using it in this way, you can cut around a drawn shape exactly $\frac{1}{4}$in (6mm) from the line without measuring. The arm also helps to steady the cutter so that it is easier to use freehand.

All this high-tech equipment is useless if it is not used properly and with confidence. The section on rotary cutting, pages 17–20, gives step-by-step instructions on how to cut the strips and squares you need for the various techniques. Just follow the pictures and all will be well.

Other Useful Items

Display Board: A piece of white felt or flannelette stretched over a board makes a good surface for placing your pieces and planning your designs, as the cut pieces will 'stick' to the fabric without pins. Work with the board upright if you can, as you get a much better idea of the effect than if the board is left lying flat on the table. A large cork or polystyrene tile also works well, but with both of these you will need pins to keep the pieces in position.

Light Box: A light box for tracing designs on to fabric can be bought from business supply shops, but it is very expensive. All you really need is a flat, clear surface that is lit from below so that the lines to be traced are highlighted through the fabric; a glass-topped table with a light placed underneath it will give the same effect. I use a square of clear perspex supported by four plastic beakers with a short strip-lighting fitment placed underneath it, completely portable and very efficient. If all else fails, tape the design to a large window, tape the fabric over the top and you will be able to see through to trace the outline; this only works well in the daytime!

BASIC TECHNIQUES

Making a sampler quilt is not particularly complex, although it does require an ability to sew and an enjoyment of combining fabrics. Nevertheless, there are some aspects which require a certain amount of expertise to ensure that the finished result is as perfect as you would like. This section looks at some of the basic techniques you need to master.

Making Templates

Many of the blocks in this sampler quilt use specific shapes which are joined together to create the design. These shapes are all given with the individual block instructions and should be traced off the page and made into templates to be used as required.

The templates can be made by tracing off each shape and transferring it on to card or special template plastic. If using card, first trace the shape on to tracing paper. When tracing straight-lined shapes such as a diamond, mark the corners with a dot and then carefully join the dots with a ruler and a sharp pencil (Figs 1a and 1b). This makes a much more accurate outline than trying to trace each line directly on to the paper. Slope the pencil at an angle of 45° to the ruler to keep the lines accurate. Mark the arrow to show the direction of the grain of the fabric. Cut out the traced shape roughly, keeping about 1/4in (6mm) outside the drawn outline (Fig 1c). Stick this on to card and then cut out the exact outline through both tracing paper and card. Try to cut just inside the drawn lines as this keeps the measurements accurate as you draw round the template on the fabric.

If using template plastic trace over the outline and grain arrow in the way described above. Cut out the template carefully with scissors, again cutting just inside the lines to keep the measurements accurate. Label each template clearly and put them all in an envelope or transparent wallet so that you can use them again.

When you get adventurous and want to draft your own patchwork blocks, draw the design accurately on graph paper first and then make templates from this following the instructions above.

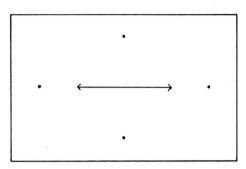

Fig 1a

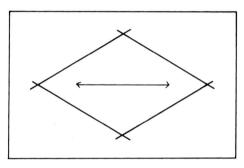

Fig 1b

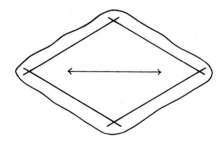

Fig 1c

Pressing

A good iron and ironing board are essential for all sewing work. Press all your fabric before you use it as creased fabric leads to inaccuracy. When pressing seams in patchwork use a dry iron as steam can distort, especially on bias seams. There are times, of course, when you actually want to distort the fabric, for example when two sides which should match do not. At such times having a steam facility on your iron is good news.

Try to resist the temptation to press seams in patchwork from the back. It seems the logical thing to do so that you can make sure the seams are all lying flat to one side. However, you could press little pleats in the fabric over the seams which you only discover when you turn the piece over to the front. These tiny, roll-over creases are hard to press out and can lead to inaccuracy. So always press from the front, guiding the seams away from the iron with your other hand so that the iron itself is pushing the seams to one side as it presses (Fig 2).

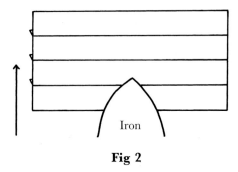

Fig 2

Setting Up The Machine

It is important to have your sewing machine and chair at the right height. An office chair might be a good investment as it can be adjusted to your personal ideal height; alternatively, firm cushions on an ordinary chair may solve any problem.

If you are short of space and cannot leave your sewing machine permanently in position, do all the preliminary cutting work first and then clear a space for the machine. Most of the machined techniques require you to sew, cut and sew in sequence so you will still need to find a space for the cutting mat once the machine is in use, but at least by then the pieces of fabric will be smaller and the whole space easier to organize.

Thread the machine ready for use. If it has an extension plate that fits on to create a larger surface, do use it as it supports the patchwork and stops it from pulling away from the needle as you stitch. Set the stitch length to a shorter stitch than required for dressmaking – about ⅔ the usual size or about fifteen stitches to the inch. This will be small enough to prevent the seams from coming undone when they are cut, but not so small that you could never unpick the stitches if required.

Many people find stitching a straight line very difficult. If you can get a ¼in (6mm) foot that fits on to your machine, it really will help. One trick is to stick a strip of masking tape on to the machine exactly ¼in (6mm) away from the needle. This makes a good edge to line your fabric against as you sew. Measure the distance from the needle by taking a piece of thin card and drawing a line exactly ¼in

(6mm) from the edge. Lift the machine pressure foot and position the needle down into the card on the drawn line. Now stick a strip of masking tape alongside the edge of the card (picture below). This should be exactly ¼in (6mm) from the needle. If you still find it difficult to stitch straight, stick a double layer of tape on to the machine ¼in (6mm) away from the needle so that there is a ridge of tape to push the fabric against as you sew. Use the point of a stitch ripper to help guide the fabric accurately while stitching.

Masking tape helps keep the ¼in (6mm) seams accurate.

TESTING FOR ACCURACY

There is a useful test to find out whether your ¼in (6mm) is accurate. The seam may be just right mathematically but because the seams are pressed to one side rather than pressed open, it makes the seams a tiny bit wider, so you need to stitch a slightly skinny ¼in (6mm) to finish up with the correct sizing. (I can hear the mathematicians shuddering as they read this, how can you have skinny seams and fat seams? Sorry, but that is what you get if you work with fabric and not with well-behaved paper.)

Take a strip of one of your fabrics 2in (5cm) wide and about 18in (45.7cm) long and cut it into three lengths (Fig 3a). Stitch these three lengths together with a ¼in (6mm) seam. Press the seams to one side, from the front of the work so that the seams are really flat (Fig 3b). Now measure the work from side to side, it should be exactly 5in (12.7cm). If it is smaller than this your seams are too wide; if it is more than 5in (12.7cm) your seams are too narrow. Try the test again, adjusting the position of your

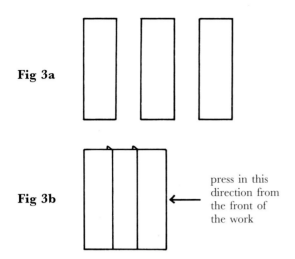

Fig 3a

Fig 3b

press in this
direction from
the front of
the work

masking tape until you get exactly the right seam allowance. Once this has been done you are set up for all your future patchwork.

Rotary Cutting

To cut the fabric place it on the mat and align the woven threads of the fabric (called the grain) with the gridlines on the mat. Position the ruler on the fabric and hold it firmly so your hand forms an arch and is not lying flat, as there is more strength in your fingers than in the flat of the hand. Hold the cutter at an angle of 45° to the mat, not leaning to one side or the other. The flatter side of the cutter should be against the side of the ruler, not the side with the assembly nut. Only snap down the safety guard when you are ready to cut (Pic 1). Left-handed users simply cut from the left side rather than from the right. Get into the habit of always cutting *away* from you,

1. Ruler and cutter are held in position ready to cut.

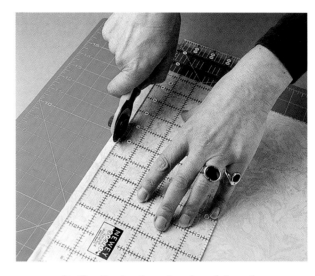

2. Cut firmly along the edge of the ruler.

3. Hold the ruler in position with the left hand.

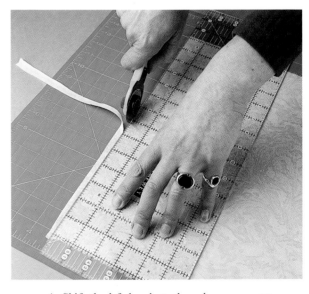

4. Shift the left hand up the ruler as you cut.

so start at the near side of the mat and begin cutting before the blade reaches the fabric, pressing down firmly and evenly in one continuous movement (Pic 2, page 17). If the ruler has a tendency to slip to one side as you cut, stop cutting and move your hand crab-like up the ruler before starting to cut again. Flip the cut edge of the fabric back so that there is a clear space of mat on which to restart cutting (Pics 3 and 4, page 17).

CUTTING STRIPS

Remember that strips cut from the width of the fabric will be stretchy, so whenever possible cut strips down the side parallel to the selvedge. If you are working with more than a couple of yards or metres of fabric, cutting from the long side of the fabric will also keep the length intact for use in borders later. So many quick machined patchwork techniques require accurately cut strips of fabric and these long lengths mean more speed and less wastage.

1 Turn the cutting mat so that the longer side runs from top to bottom to give a longer cutting distance. If the piece of fabric is too long for the mat, fold it carefully as many times as needed to make it fit on to the cutting mat with the selvedge edges *exactly* on top of each other. It may help to press the layers together with an iron, but do not use pins in case you accidentally run over a pin with the cutter and ruin the blade. Place the fabric on the mat with the folded edge along a horizontal gridline (Pic 1). This is very important to avoid getting V-shapes in the final long strip.

2 Place the ruler on one of the vertical gridlines on the mat and trim off the selvedges (Pic 2). To cut a strip of a measured width use the marked measurements at the top and bottom of the mat. I never trust my sums, so I actually count the number of inches along the top markings on the mat. Move the ruler to this position, hold it firmly and cut along its edge. Before moving the ruler, check that all the layers have been completely cut through. If not, re-cut the whole strip rather than saw at the offending section.

3 Lift the ruler and reposition it for cutting the next strip (Pic 3). Continue to cut until the necessary number of strips has been cut (Pic 4).

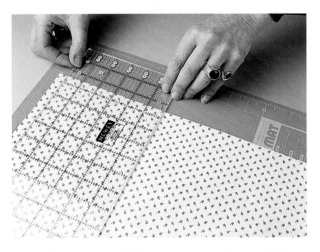

1: Folded layers of fabric are placed with the fold(s) lined up with a horizontal gridline on the mat.

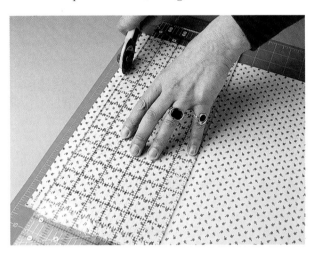

2: Selvedges are trimmed away, using a vertical gridline on the mat as a guide.

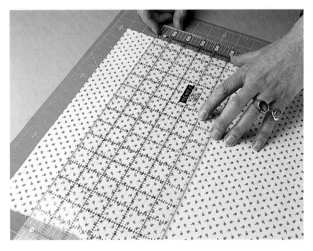

3: The ruler is repositioned at the correct distance for the strip width by using the mat markings.

4: Continue to move the ruler across the fabric and cut strips in the same way, using the mat markings as measurements.

AN ALTERNATIVE METHOD FOR CUTTING STRIPS

When cutting strips or drawing a grid for quick pieced triangles, measurements like $3\frac{7}{8}$in (9.8cm) are quite common. It is all too easy to mis-measure when using the mat markings as a guide. Instead, after trimming the selvedges, turn the mat through 180° without disturbing the fabric, or walk around the mat to the other side if necessary. Start cutting from the left-hand side instead of from the right. If you are left-handed just reverse these directions. Pass the ruler over the cut edge until the fabric edge lines up with the required measurement on the ruler itself, ignore the markings on the mat except as a general indication that the ruler is staying truly vertical (Pic 1). Cut along the ruler's right side and remove the cut

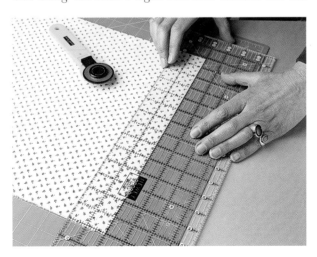

1. Start cutting from the left-hand side.

strip (Pic 2). Move the ruler across the fabric until the new cut edge matches up with the required measurement on the ruler and cut once more (Pic 3). Continue to do this across the fabric as many times as required.

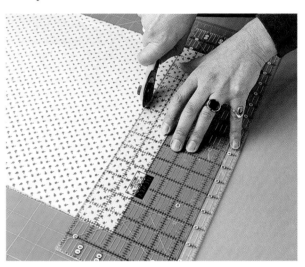

2. Pass the ruler over the fabric edge to the required width.

3. Cut along the ruler's right side and remove the strip.

CUTTING A SQUARE

If the fabric will fit on to the mat without hanging over the edge, place it down with the grain parallel to the mat's gridlines. Straighten one edge of the fabric by lining the ruler up with a vertical gridline and cutting against it. Without moving the fabric, cut a second vertical line at the desired distance from the first one – I always count the squares to make sure I have got it right. Turn the mat through 90° and trim the other two sides of the square in the same way.

If the piece of fabric is too big for the mat, you

could cut out the square roughly first and then trim it on the mat as described above or alternatively use one of the large square rulers. Place a corner of the fabric on the mat, matching the fabric grain with the mat's gridlines. Position the square ruler on it with about ½in (1.2cm) of fabric to spare on two sides.

1. Trim two sides of the fabric with a square ruler.

2. Move the ruler over the cut edges.

3. Trim the remaining two sides of fabric.

Trim along these sides with the cutter (Pic 1). Turn the square so that the diagonal line marked 0 is at the trimmed corner. Move it across the cut edges until the chosen measurement on the two sides of the ruler lines up with the cut edges (Pic 2). Trim the remaining two sides to complete the square (Pic 3). In this way the square is cut with very little waste.

USING THE SEAM GUIDE

Once you get used to using the rotary equipment you may well find it frustrating to slowly cut round shapes with scissors. When preparing for American pieced patchwork blocks, like Card Trick, I draw around each template and then, by eye, cut the extra ¼in (6mm) seam allowance needed with a small rotary cutter. This is not as risky as it sounds, as the width of the seam allowance does not have to be totally accurate. The guide arm attachment for the rotary cutter gives greater accuracy and makes the cutter steadier.

1 Fix the black arm at a distance of ¼in (6mm) from the blade. If you have a small cutter, this is ideal for the job.

2 With the wrong side upwards, place the fabric on the mat so that the drawn template shapes can be seen. Smooth down the fabric to make cutting easier.

3 Run the cutter around each shape with the black arm running exactly on the drawn outline. The blade will automatically cut at a distance of ¼in (6mm) from the line.

Using a guide arm to cut a ¼in (6mm) seam allowance.

Do not think that you *have* to use this gadget. It may suit the less patient among you who like to whizz through everything. But if you enjoy the quiet tranquillity of cutting each piece as you sit, then that has to be the best way for you.

MAKING THE BLOCKS

You are now almost ready to start making the blocks for your sampler quilt.
Each design and technique you will need is fully described, with step-by-step
instructions, and with each one I have tried to give some ideas for selecting
colours and fabrics. If you look at the quilt photographs throughout the
book, most made by first-time quilters, you will get some ideas for your
own colour schemes.

The blocks are presented in sequence so that the skills learned in one design are
built upon in the following block. Probably the best way to use the book is to work
through the block instructions, one by one. However if, for example, you absolutely
hate all machine work, then just leave out all the machine blocks and make twice
as many hand-pieced blocks. In the same way, if you find a block that you feel
is not for you, then just leave it out. It is, after all, *your* quilt and you are
allowed to pick and choose.

The advantage of making and quilting the blocks individually and then assembling
them at the end is that you can decide how many to make. Whether they finish up
as a huge king-size quilt, a cot quilt or just a series of cushions is up to you.

Detail from a quilt made by Sue Fitzgerald.

ENGLISH PATCHWORK

TUMBLING BLOCKS

Patchwork over papers is a traditional English method of patchwork. Many people believe – incorrectly – that hand-stitching hexagons is the only form of patchwork there is, whilst those more experienced in quilt-making often see the hexagon as a design cliché lacking in imagination and creativity. Although this can be true, I have seen some beautiful hexagon quilts made in recent years where scraps of many fabrics have been blended and balanced for colour and design. These quilts are destined to

become heirlooms, passed on and treasured for their looks as well as for their nostalgic content. The almost mindless repetition involved in this method is wonderfully soothing and therapeutic to do, and I have seen many a quilter abandon a challenging project in times of stress, unhappiness or sheer fatigue to take up a piece of English patchwork over papers.

It is not just hexagons that are stitched in this way, but any geometric shape that does not fit neatly into squares and rows, such as diamonds, octagons and equilateral triangles. The papers give a rigid outline to the shapes which makes it easy to join them together with great accuracy. Once completed, the papers are all removed and can be re-used on another project.

For the sampler quilt I have chosen a design called Tumbling Blocks, an arrangement of diamonds that gives the illusion of a three-dimensional tower of blocks. It is also known as Baby's Blocks.

COLOUR CHOICES

The design is made up of groups of three diamonds arranged to form a hexagon. To obtain the three-dimensional effect use three different fabrics: one dark, one light and one medium. Place the three fabrics alongside each other to check that one stands out as being lighter and another is definitely darker. The third fabric will lie between these two extremes as a medium tone. The contrasts do not have to be great but should be enough to register on the eye, or the illusion of a tower of bricks will be lost. Half-closing your eyes when looking at the fabrics will help you see the difference in tone. A fourth fabric is required for the background on which the tower sits. You may like to use the same background fabric for all of your blocks to give continuity to the quilt, or you may decide to vary the background from block to block. A plain fabric is the obvious choice, but also consider a small print or textured design, even a small check or spot will read from a distance as plain but could add interest.

The possibilities are there for you to make your own personal choice. Do not rush it: place the three fabrics for the Tumbling Blocks in the middle of your background choice and consider the effect. If you're not sure, try another background and then go back to the first. If you're still unsure, make the Tumbling Blocks first, then arrange them on various fabrics to see what looks best. All the time you are sewing the diamonds you can be quietly thinking about the options for the background and could well come to a decision before you get anywhere near the final stage.

CONSTRUCTION

1 Make a template by tracing the diamond shape from Fig 1, cutting it out and sticking it on to card, or use template plastic, see page 15 for instructions on making templates.

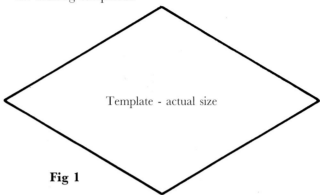

Template - actual size

Fig 1

2 Using a really sharp pencil to keep the shape accurate, draw round the template on to thick paper – the cartridge paper in children's drawing books is ideal. Do not use card as it is too thick. Mark the corners of the diamonds by continuing the drawn lines to just beyond the template corners so that they cross. This cross marks the exact corner and will make cutting out more accurate (Fig 2).

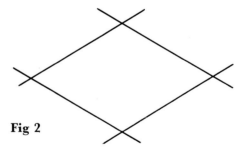

Fig 2

3 Cut out eighteen paper diamonds, cutting just inside the drawn lines to prevent the shape becoming larger than the original diamond.
4 On the wrong side of each fabric, pin six paper shapes, following the straight grain of the fabric and leaving a $\frac{1}{4}$in (6mm) gap around each paper as shown in Fig 3.

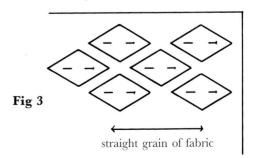

Fig 3

straight grain of fabric

5 Cut around each paper adding a ¼in (6mm) seam allowance on all sides. This does not have to be carefully measured and marked as it is not critical if you are a little generous. However, try to avoid cutting a seam allowance less than ¼in (6mm) as this makes tacking difficult. The points at the long corners can be shortened to leave a ¼in (6mm) margin of fabric beyond the paper (Fig 4).

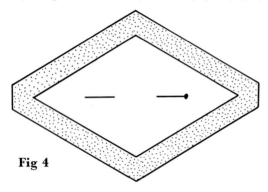

Fig 4

6 Thread a needle – I use either crewel needles or Sharps size 8 or 9 – with tacking thread. Begin with a knot and tack fabric to paper by folding the seam allowance tightly over the paper and stitching it down. The corner of folded fabric extending beyond the diamond can be ignored at this stage (Fig 5). Turn the tacked shape over and check that the corners exactly outline the shape of the paper beneath it (Fig 6). Remove the pins.

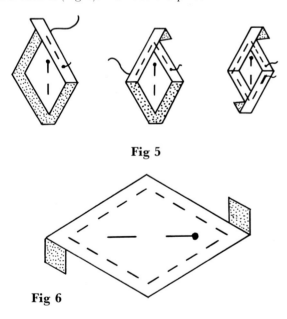

Fig 5

Fig 6

7 Arrange one light, one medium and one dark diamond in the desired design (Fig 7). I have put the lightest fabric horizontally across the top of each block, but you may like to arrange them differently. As long as all six blocks are identical you can place

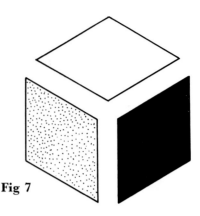

Fig 7

the diamonds however you like. Thread a needle with no more than 18in (45.7cm) of toning thread. If stitching two different coloured fabrics together, match the thread to the darker fabric as it is always less obvious than the lighter.

Take two diamond shapes and place them right sides together ready to sew. If one edge seems longer than the other, (this happens more often than you would think, so do not blame yourself) place them so that the shorter edge is lying on top as you work. As you sew the top layer stretches, just as it does on a sewing machine, so you can ease the shorter edge to fit the longer. Fix the corner you are working towards with a pin (Fig 8) so that as you sew the two corners will match exactly.

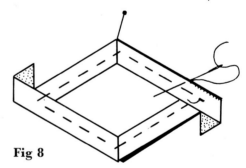

Fig 8

8 Starting with a double stitch to secure the thread, oversew with small even stitches, making sure that the two sets of corners match exactly.

SHIRLEY STOCKS

'Making the sampler quilt really increased my understanding and confidence in choosing and matching colours and patterns. I found the hand-quilting on the deep borders very hard to master but convinced myself that it was character building.'

The stitches should be about the same distance apart as small machine stitches. If you stitch too closely you can weaken the fabric and make almost a satin stitch effect which will prevent the finished seam from lying flat (Fig 9).

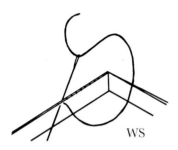

Fig 9

As you sew the corners, push the seam allowances to one side so that they stick out beyond the edges (Fig 10). Once the papers are removed these extra flaps dovetail in with each other without adding extra bulk. Do not be tempted to trim down these flaps as this can weaken the seams. Finish sewing with a double stitch and cut the thread, leaving about 1/4in (6mm) for safety.

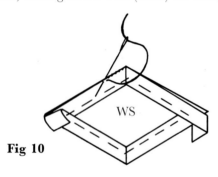

Fig 10

9 Open out the two diamonds and attach diamond three in the same way, sewing another double stitch at the centre of all three diamonds to strengthen it.

10 Assemble all six hexagons in this way and join them together to make the tower shape (Fig 11). Press before removing the papers so that the outer seam allowances remain turned under. Remove tacking by undoing the final stitch and pulling firmly on the knot to pull the tacking thread out in one length. The papers can then be lifted out and stored. Tack around the edges of the tower shape to keep the seam allowances in place, folding back any flaps that are sticking out under the main shape and including these in the tacking.

11 Cut a 13in (33cm) square of fabric for the background. Although the finished size will be 12½in (31.7cm) square, when one fabric is stitched on to another (known as appliqué), the bottom

fabric often draws up slightly to finish up smaller than when you started. By using a 13in (33cm) square it can be accurately trimmed to 12½in (31.7cm) once the tower has been stitched in place.

12 Place the tower centrally on the background fabric. It helps if you fold the square in four and crease lightly with your fingers, the creases make guidelines for positioning the tower. Pin or tack the tower on to the background square.

13 Using a shade of thread to match the tower and not the background, sew the tower on to the background, keeping the stitches small and even. Sew a double stitch at each corner to secure it (Fig 12).

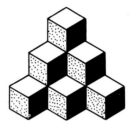
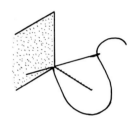

Fig 11   **Fig 12**

14 Before an appliquéd shape is quilted its thickness can be reduced by cutting the background fabric away from behind the appliqué. This is not compulsory and if you are nervous about doing this, leave it. However, it does make the whole piece easier to quilt and allows the piece to lie flatter.

Turn the block to the back and, with your fingers, just pull away the backing from the appliqué at the centre. Make a small cut in the backing fabric. Once you have done this, carefully cut away the backing up to 1/4in (6mm) from the stitching line of the appliqué, leaving the appliqué itself intact (Fig 13).

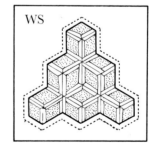

Fig 13

15 Trim the finished block to an exact 12½in (31.7cm) square and add the framing sashing strips, see page 110 for instructions. If you have not yet chosen the sashing fabric, leave the block until you have completed enough other blocks to help you make your decision.

MACHINED STRIP PATCHWORK

RAIL FENCE

This block is a traditional strip design which, in the past, has been made by hand using a template for each strip. We can now use a rotary cutter and ruler to cut the strips and a sewing machine to stitch the block quickly and accurately.

The design is made by sewing together three long strips of different fabrics and then re-cutting this band into squares. The squares are then arranged and joined together to make the block. The project on page 135 uses Rail Fence blocks to make a quillow.

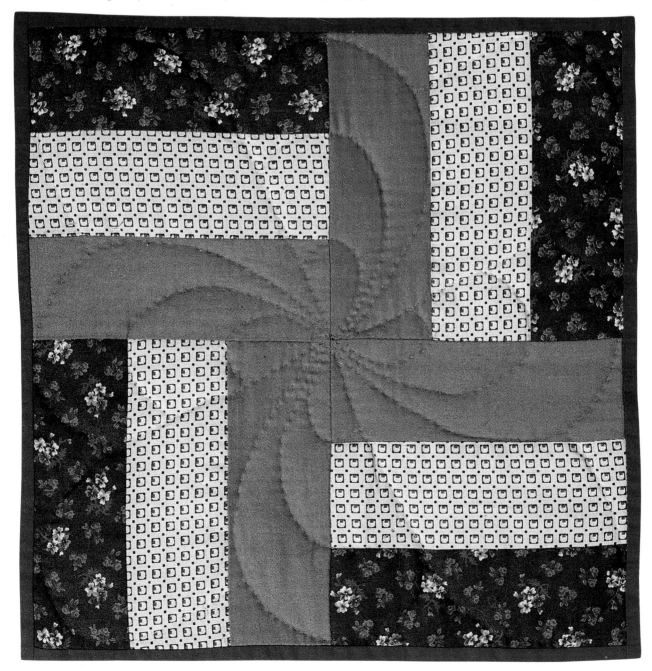

COLOUR CHOICES

For this block you need three fabrics. The same combination of fabrics used in Tumbling Blocks (page 22) could be used again or a new selection made. Fold the fabrics into narrow strips and place them next to each other on a flat surface so that you can see how effective they look together. If you are unsure about the effect, cut four strips of each fabric measuring 1/2 x 1 1/2in (1.2 x 3.8cm) and play around with them, arranging them in various combinations until you get the best effect. Stick the chosen arrangement on to card or paper.

CONSTRUCTION

1 From each fabric cut one strip measuring 2 1/2in (6.3cm) wide and 28in (71.1cm) long (Fig 1). If you are trying to cut your strips parallel to the selvedge and cannot cut a strip 28in (71.1cm) long, cut two 14in (35.5cm) long strips of each fabric instead. See page 18 for instructions on cutting strips.

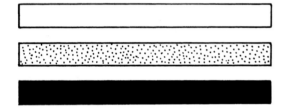

Fig 1

2 Set the stitch length on your sewing machine to about 2/3 the size of the usual dressmaking stitch, small enough to prevent the seams from coming undone when the strips are cut across, but not so small that you could never unpick the stitches if you had to. See page 16 for setting up the machine.

Be careful to ensure that the sewn seams are a scant 1/4in (6mm). A strip of masking tape stuck on to the machine plate at the correct distance from the needle can provide a useful guide.

Stitch the three strips together. I do not use pins, but stop every 3 to 4in (7.6 to 10.1cm) and line up the next section of fabric edges as I go. Try not to stretch the strips, but guide them gently, using small scissors or the point of a seam ripper to keep the edges in position. Alternate the direction you sew the strips to keep the band straight not slightly rippled (Fig 2).

3 Press the band from the front with the seams all in one direction (Fig 3). See page 15 for general advice on pressing.

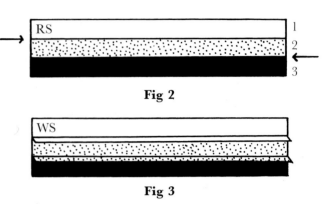

Fig 2

Fig 3

4 Place the fabric band horizontally on the cutting board, lining up the top edge with one of the horizontal markings on the board. If you are lucky the band will be perfect and lie flat, although it is more likely to have a slightly wavy or rippled effect, the result of joining together three different fabrics. You cannot help this so just place the band as flat as possible and continue.

Measure the width of the band. If you have stitched an accurate scant 1/4in (6mm) the band should be 6 1/2in (16.5cm). Using the rotary ruler and cutter, trim one end of the band to straighten it and cut four sections each 6 1/2in (16.5cm) long, to make four squares (Fig 4).

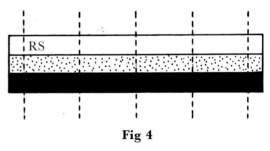

Fig 4

NB If your band does not measure 6 1/2in (16.5cm), even if it is only 1/8in (3mm) out, take the measurement you have and cut the four squares to match it. This way you will have true squares, even if they are slightly more or less than intended. You can make adjustments later on if necessary.

DAPHNE GREEN

'This quilt nearly became another unfinished statistic because of the problems I had with the borders. Still, with a great deal of help and encouragement it was finally completed!'

5 Arrange the four squares to make the block design (Fig 5). Pin and machine-stitch the top two squares together with a ¼in (6mm) seam. If you

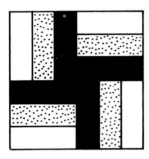

Fig 5

place the pins at right angles to the seams you will be able to stitch right up to each pin before removing it (Fig 6).

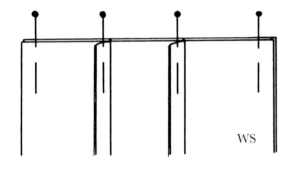

Fig 6

If the two edges do not match exactly and one is shorter than the other, pin and stitch with the shorter edge on top, as this will stretch slightly as you stitch and should ease the problem. Press the seams to one side from the front of the joined squares.

6 Pin and machine-stitch the second pair of squares. Press the seams in the opposite direction to the first half (Fig 7).

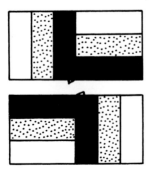

Fig 7

7 Join the two halves by stitching across with a ¼in (6mm) seam, taking care to match the centre seams. Pressing the centre seams of each half in opposite directions will help you to match them accurately, as they lock into each other as you sew. Pin diagonally as this helps to keep both sets of seam allowances flat while stitching (Fig 8). The final long seam can be pressed to one side or, if this makes it too bulky, press the seam open (Fig 9).

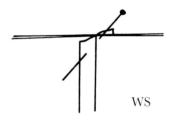

WS

Fig 8

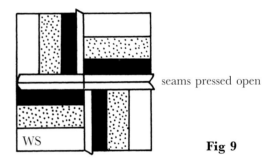

seams pressed open

WS

Fig 9

8 Trim the block to an exact 12½in (31.7cm) square. If it is too small, cut it down a little more and add an extra border with a fabric that frames the block well. See page 109 for instructions on trimming and bordering blocks. This border can then be trimmed down to make the completed block exactly 12½in (31.7cm) square. If you have chosen the fabric for the framing sashing strips, add them, following the instructions on page 110. If not, just leave your decision until you have made a few more blocks.

MAPLE LEAF

It was seeing the quilt collection in the American Museum at Claverton Manor near Bath that started my life-long love affair with quilts and quilt-making. I had only ever seen museum exhibits of Victorian hexagon or octagon quilts – often unfin-ished – and till then had no idea what a rich mix of shape and colour had been established in traditional American quilts.

The Americans view the idea of piecing patchwork using papers as near madness. They have their own

technique of hand-piecing that evolved when the early settlers from Europe found themselves facing cruel winters without sufficient warm covers. They needed to make thick blankets as quickly as possible from the few scraps and rags available, so they joined squares, rectangles and strips into a blanket-shaped piece. Another similar shape was made and a filling of shredded rags, wool and scraps was placed between the two to give some warmth. To keep the filling in place an even running stitch was made through all the layers.

In time the makers of these quilts used the traditions of quilt-making that had been brought with them from Europe to turn the random piecing of patches into regular designs. The designs took the form of squares, called blocks, of sizes varying from 10in (25.4cm) to 16in (40.7cm) or 18in (45.7cm), which were repeated and joined to make quilts. There are now hundreds of traditional block designs, many appearing in different areas of the United States under a variety of names. Their names reflect the life and times of those early settlers: Bear's Paws, Goose Tracks, Hovering Hawks. Others show a religious influence: Jacob's Ladder, Hosannah, Steps to the Altar. Some blocks have been named after a person, which makes you wonder who they were.

The stitching in these blocks did not need to be as strong as that in English patchwork because the quilting stitches, which crossed and recrossed the quilt through all the layers, reinforced the fabrics and took the strain off the linking stitches. The traditional American method of patchwork uses templates to mark the fabrics, the pieces are joined by matching up and stitching along the drawn lines.

The block I have chosen to introduce this most commonly used hand technique is the Maple Leaf. It is a design based on nine squares, some of which are divided into smaller shapes. Any pattern which has these nine basic squares is called a Nine-Patch and many Nine-Patch designs can be found amongst the traditional patchwork blocks. A border strip has been added to the left side and along the bottom of the block. I especially like the diagonal slant to this block as it gives a lovely feeling of movement when repeated on a large quilt. It is ideal for a corner block in a sampler quilt where it draws the eye from the corner into the main quilt (Fig 1).

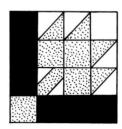

Fig 1

COLOUR CHOICES

This simple block needs two fabrics, one for the leaf itself and one for the background, plus a third fabric for the border strips. The corner square at the bottom left corner of the design could be made from the leaf fabric, the background fabric or another fabric altogether. Do not think that because you are piecing a leaf, it has to be a correct leaf colour, the *shape* is a maple leaf, the colours can be whatever suits your own quilt. You do not need a large square of background fabric as you did for the Tumbling Blocks. Here every piece is cut to shape and joined with its neighbour to form the complete block.

CONSTRUCTION

1 Make templates by tracing the five shapes from Fig 2 page 34, cutting them out and sticking them on to card, or use template plastic, see page 15 for instructions on making templates.

2 On the wrong side of each fabric, draw accurately around the templates using a sharp marking pencil. This marks the sewing line. Allow at least ½in (1.2cm) between each drawn outline so that a seam allowance of ¼in (6mm) can be added to each shape when cutting out (Fig 3). For the leaf you will need three of square A, four of triangle B and one of stem C. Save space by arranging the shapes on the fabric as shown in Fig 4. For the background you need one of square A, four of triangle B and two of triangle D. For the border you need two of rectangle E and one of square A.

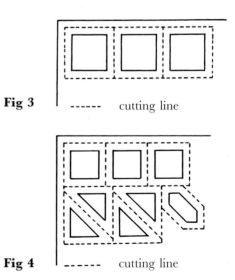

Fig 3   ------ cutting line

Fig 4   ------ cutting line

3 Cut out each shape to include the ¼in (6mm) seam allowance, either by eye or more accurately by using a ¼in (6mm) rule known as a quilter's quarter or a seamwheel, see Basic Equipment page

MARION EDWARDS

'My memory of my sampler quilt is of the wonderful scenery of a New Zealand holiday. The colours seemed appropriate too. It's amazing how many blocks will fit into the handbag for whiling away the time on long journeys!'

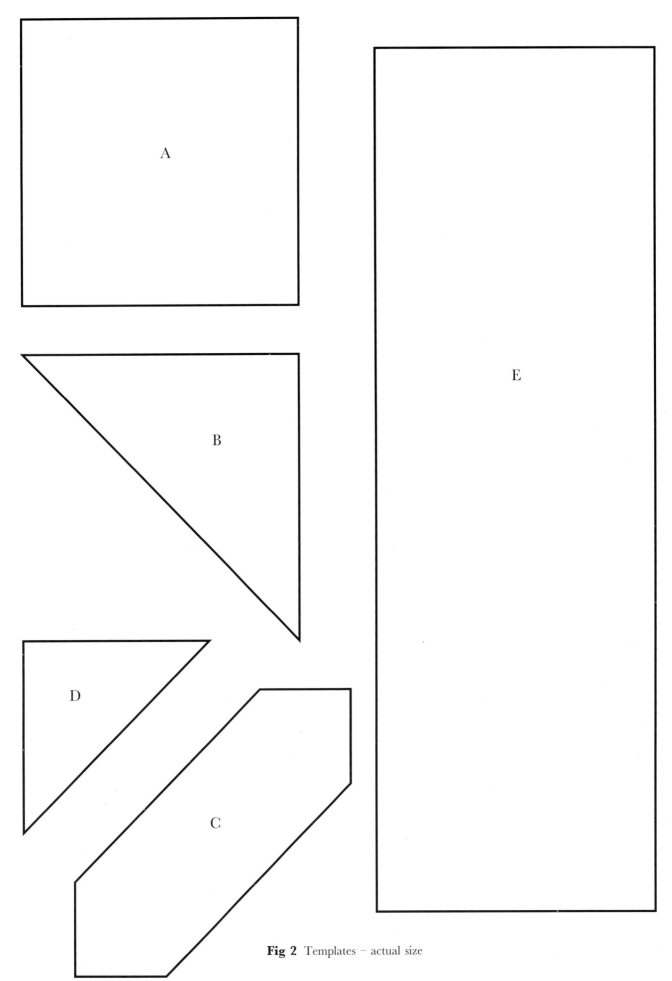

Fig 2 Templates – actual size

10. I like to cut on a board with a small rotary cutter with the seam guide set ¼in (6mm) from the blade. In time you get used to judging this distance and you may find it quicker to cut without extra markings. As with English patchwork, the exact width of the seam allowance is not critical, so judging by eye is perfectly acceptable if you feel comfortable doing it this way.

4 Arrange the cut pieces on a flat surface or pin them in position on a polystyrene tile or display board. Final adjustments to the design can be made at this stage.

5 Do not try to assemble the leaf and then join on the background pieces. Instead, assemble each of the nine squares in the following way (Fig 5).

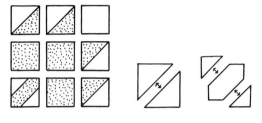

Fig 5

Place the first two triangles together, right sides facing. The pencil markings will be on the outside and must be positioned exactly on top of each other as they indicate the sewing lines. Align the starting points of the sewing lines by pushing a pin through both layers of fabric until the head is on the surface of the top fabric. Repeat this to mark the finishing point (Fig 6). Reposition the pins at right angles to the seam. Add more pins along the seamline, matching the marked lines (Fig 7).

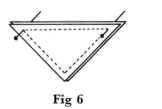

Fig 6

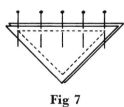

Fig 7

6 Starting with a double stitch, sew along the pencilled line with small running stitches about the same length as machine stitches, loading several stitches on to the needle at a time. Begin each run of stitches with a backstitch to secure the work firmly. Finish the seam exactly at the end of the marked line with several backstitches (Fig 8).

Do not sew into the seam allowances, these are left free so that once the block is complete the seams may be pressed to one side. They are never

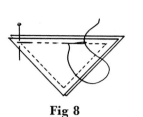

Fig 8

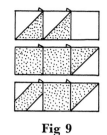

Fig 9

pressed open, as the hand-sewn stitches are not strong enough.

7 Once all nine squares are assembled, sew together the horizontal rows of three squares, pinning and matching the seams as before (Fig 9). Join the top two rows by placing them right sides together, matching seams. Push a pin exactly through the seams and corners on each piece. Reposition the pins at right angles to the seams and add more along the seamlines, matching the marked lines (Fig 10). As before, sew together without sewing into the seam allowances, instead, sew up to each seam and make a backstitch. Pass the needle through the seam allowances to the other side. Backstitch again and continue sewing (Fig 11). Join on the third row in the same way.

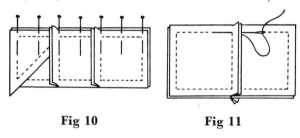

Fig 10   **Fig 11**

8 Attach a border strip to the side of the block using the same method. Join the remaining square and border strip together. Finally sew these along the bottom edge to complete the block.

9 Measure the block, it should be 12½in (31.7cm) square. If it needs trimming, trim away on the two border sides *only* so that you do not trim off the corners of the maple leaf (Fig 12).

10 Add the framing sashing strips if you are ready to, see page 110 for instructions.

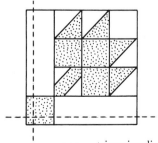

Fig 12   ----- trimming line if necessary

TRIP AROUND THE WORLD

This simple design of squares is a traditional pattern frequently found in Amish quilts. The Amish are a religious sect now found mainly in Pennsylvania, Ohio and Indiana in the United States. They left Alsace, on the borders of France and Germany, to avoid persecution in the eighteenth century, and founded their own farming communities in the New World based on their beliefs. They live a simple life set apart as much as possible from the surrounding world. They have no connection by

telephone or electricity lines, nor water or gas pipes. They are excellent farmers, sharing basic equipment which is pulled by horses or man-powered. The communities follow a strict code in the way they decorate their houses and in their clothing. Everything is simple and plain, using Nature's colours only. They make all their family clothes, using black, white and grey, browns, greens, blues and mauves. The dresses are very simple and are worn with a white bonnet and a black or white cape and apron. No fancy frills or even patterned fabrics are used in their clothing nor in the quilts for which they are famous. The simple designs use a mixture of clear, plain colours and have a strength and elegance that is enhanced by wonderful hand-quilting. Amish quilts, especially antique ones, have been likened to modern abstract art and are now collectors' items, commanding very high prices.

The design Trip Around The World is based on simple squares using several colours. The central square represents the world and each surrounding row is a new colour, making a diamond design around the single central square (Fig 1). There must

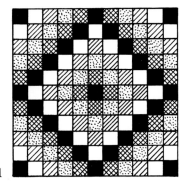

Fig 1

be an odd number of squares in each row, such as nine, eleven or fifteen so that there is one square in the centre of the block for the focus (the world). For the 12in (30.5cm) block in the sampler quilt I have used seven squares in each row so that the piecing is not too fiddly, making a total of forty-nine squares.

COLOUR CHOICES

If you wish you can use seven colours, changing for each circuit of squares. This can look very busy so you may wish to limit the fabrics to four or five; Fig 2 shows three different arrangements of squares, to give you some ideas. Most books suggest that when planning the colours for a design like this you should draw out the block on squared paper and colour it in to see the different effects. This is fine, but I find it very difficult to relate the shaded pencil

Fig 2

colours to actual fabric. Ideally you should just cut lots of fabric squares and play with them, but this inevitably leads to waste; also it takes a strong person to discard twenty cut squares of one fabric in favour of another because the original idea did not work as well as you had hoped. I favour a compromise: from each fabric cut a strip ½in (1.2cm) wide and 10 to 12in (25.4 to 30.5cm) long. From these cut off ½in (1.2cm) squares. Now play with these small pieces until you find the design you like best. There is little wastage using these narrow strips and you will get a good idea of what the completed block will look like. Either stick the chosen arrangement on to card or paper or draw a plan of it on squared paper to keep as a reference. Using a felt board is ideal, as the fabric squares can be placed on it and they will stay in position without pinning, see Basic Equipment page 10.

CONSTRUCTION

1 From your chosen fabrics cut strips 2¼in (5.7cm) wide. The length of each strip will vary according to how many 2¼in (5.7cm) squares are needed for your design. Place each strip horizontally on the cutting board, lining the top long edge with a horizontal marking line on the board. Cut pieces from each strip to make squares 2¼in (5.7cm) in size (Fig 3).

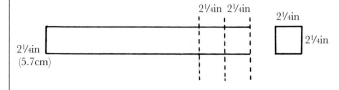

Fig 3

2 Arrange the squares in your chosen design and check that it looks as good as it seemed when you made it with the tiny squares.

3 Stitching an exact $\frac{1}{4}$in (6mm) seam at all times, machine together the squares from the top row of the design. Position the squares by matching them edge to edge so that there is no need to pin them together. If you use a smaller stitch (about $\frac{2}{3}$ normal size) there is no need to secure the ends by reversing the stitching.

If the design is symmetrical (and it should be!), row one should be the same as row seven, row two the same as row six and row three the same as row five. Row four is the centre row and is unique (Fig 4).

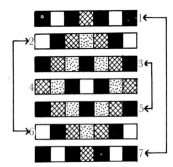

Fig 4

Consider streamlining your stitching and saving time and thread by sewing each pair of identical rows at the same time. Stitch together the first pair of squares in row one, stopping at the last stitch on the fabric. Take the identical pair of squares from row seven and place them right sides together matching the edges. Without lifting the pressure foot, slip this pair under the front of the foot and continue sewing (Fig 5).

A short length of machined stitches will separate each pair of squares. Remove the squares from the machine and cut the threads to separate them. Open out the joined squares from row one and place the third square in position. Stitch down this seam and continue stitching the identical seam for row seven (Fig 6).

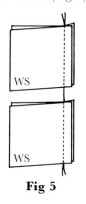

Fig 5

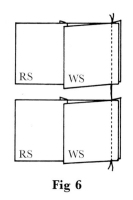

Fig 6

Remove the pieces from the machine and cut the threads to separate them. Continue to do this for each square that you add, stitching row one first and then row seven. Do the same for rows two and six and for rows three and five. This technique is called stringing or chaining. If you find it simpler to join each row individually, do so – use the method you are comfortable with.

4 Press from the front, ironing the seams of row one in one direction and those in row two the opposite way. Continue to press each row with seams alternately pressed to the right and left.

5 Pin together rows one and two, matching the seams carefully. This is made easier by the pressed seams which lock into each other (Fig 7). Pin diagonally across the seam allowances to keep them flat while stitching (Fig 8).

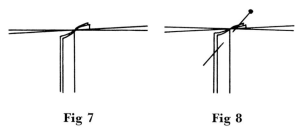

Fig 7   **Fig 8**

6 If the squares do not all match each other and a little 'easing' has to be done, stitch with the shorter edge on top, as this will stretch as you sew. Stitch rows one and row two together. Continue to pin and stitch each row until the block is completed.

7 Press from the front with the seams to one side as before. If the seams are too bulky, press these final long seams open from the back of the work.

8 Measure the completed block, it should be slightly more than 12½in (31.7cm) square and will need to be centred and trimmed down on all four sides to an exact 12½in (31.7cm) square. See page 109 for instructions on trimming the blocks.

9 Add the final sashing strips if you are ready to, see page 110 for instructions.

CHRIS MUNDY

'The quilt includes some of my favourite things: tones of blue, decoy ducks and of course patchwork and quilting. It won a silver cup as best entry in the handicraft section at the local flower show. Flushed with success, I have now embarked on another sampler quilt.'

CARD TRICK

This block uses only two templates, fewer than the Maple Leaf, but the pieces are smaller so there is more work involved. When I made my own sampler quilt I made the finished size of the Card Trick block exactly 12in (30.5cm), but I altered the size to a 9in (22.8cm) block with an added surrounding border for the students in case the completed blocks finished up a little bigger than planned. Trimming the block down to size would have cut off all those lovely points around the outside edges and spoiled

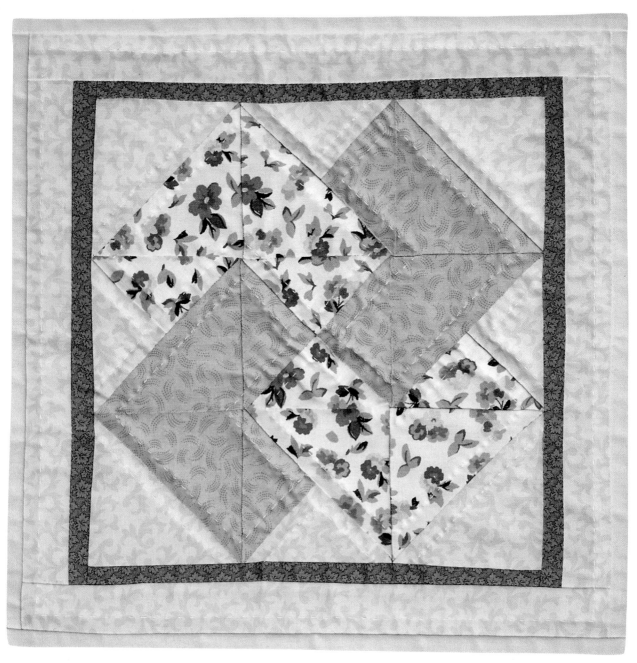

the effect. Please don't misunderstand me – I did not assume that everyone's block would be inaccurate. This was just a contingency plan so that if any block *was* too big, it would not matter. When you are a beginner I feel you need every bit of help available. Also I liked the smaller scale of the 9in (22.8cm) block, and wished I had made mine that size (Fig 1).

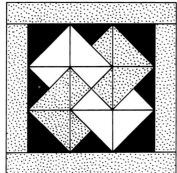

extra border

Fig 1

The templates here are for a 12in (30.5cm) block, but if you prefer the smaller version it is very easy to draft your own templates. The block is based on nine squares, three rows of three squares, which is known as a Nine-Patch. To make a 9in (22.8cm) block, each square needs to measure 3 x 3in (7.6 x 7.6cm). Draw a 3in (7.6cm) square on graph paper or template plastic, keeping the lines as accurate as possible. Divide the square with a diagonal line (Fig 2). One of the resulting triangles is used as the larger template, A. Draw another diagonal line from one

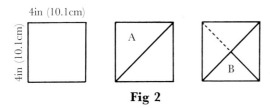

4in (10.1cm)

4in (10.1cm)

A

B

Fig 2

corner, stopping at the centre point so that the second large triangle is now divided into two. Either of these two smaller triangles is template B. If working on graph paper, cut roughly around the square, stick it on to card and then cut the two triangular templates A and B from it. See page 15 for instructions on making templates.

COLOUR CHOICES

The Card Trick block is given its name because it looks like a handful of playing cards spread out in a fan shape. There are four 'cards' made from two fabrics placed alternately, although four different fabrics can be used. Another fabric is needed for the

background. As with the Maple Leaf, this background is not just a large square on to which the cards are stitched. Instead, every piece is cut to shape and joined with its neighbour to make the block. The 'card' fabrics need to balance each other in their density of colour. In other words, you do not want one colour that is much stronger than the others. Arrange the 'card' fabrics in a cross shape on a piece of the background fabric. Stand back and half close your eyes. If one fabric seems to dominate, change it. It is easier to achieve a balance if you just use two fabrics for the cards, as in Fig 1. The background can be dark, as in Fig 1, or much lighter. You may, of course, use one fabric throughout the sampler quilt for all the backgrounds of the blocks. Remember that with the 9in (22.8cm) block an edging border of at least 1¹/₂in (3.8cm) finished width has to be added to increase it to the required 12in (30.5cm) block, so the fabric for this also has to be considered. Any extra borders around blocks like this should not be of the same fabric as the sashing strips, so if you have not made a decision on the sashing fabric, you may need to before you can go much further.

CONSTRUCTION

1 Make card templates by tracing triangles A and B from Fig 3, cutting them out and sticking them on to card, or use template plastic. If you want to

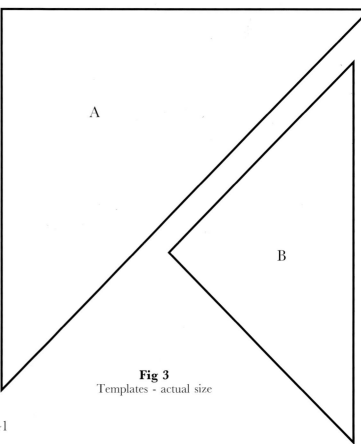

A

B

Fig 3
Templates - actual size

make the smaller block draft your own templates as explained earlier, see page 15 for instructions on making templates.

2 On the wrong side of each fabric draw accurately around the templates using a sharp marking pencil. This marks the sewing line. Allow at least ¹/₂in (1.2cm) between each drawn outline so that the seam allowance of ¹/₄in (6mm) can be added to each shape when cutting out.

If you are using two fabrics for the 'cards' you will need four of triangle A and four of triangle B from each fabric. (If using four fabrics you need two of each triangle from each fabric.) You also need four of each triangle from the background fabric. Save space by arranging the shapes on the fabric as shown in Fig 4.

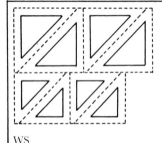

Fig 4   WS

3 Cut out each shape to include the ¹/₄in (6mm) seam allowance, either by eye or more accurately by using a ¹/₄in (6mm) rule known as a quilter's quarter or a seamwheel, see Basic Equipment page 10. I like to cut on a board with a small rotary cutter with the seam guide set ¹/₄in (6mm) from the blade. In time you get used to judging this distance, and as the exact width of the seam allowance is not critical in American piecing judging by eye is perfectly acceptable if you feel comfortable doing it this way.

4 Arrange the cut pieces on a flat surface or pin them in position on a polystyrene tile or board. Final adjustments to the design can be made at this stage.

5 Do not try to assemble the 'cards' and then join on the background pieces. Instead, assemble each of the nine squares in the following way (Fig 5). Place the first two triangles together with right sides facing. The pencil markings will be on the outside

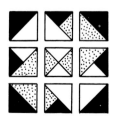

Fig 5

and must be positioned exactly on top of each other as they indicate the sewing lines. Align the starting points of the sewing lines by pushing a pin through both layers of fabric until the head is on the surface of the top fabric. Repeat this to mark the finishing point (Fig 6). Reposition the pins at right angles to the seam. Add more pins along the seamline, matching the marked lines (Fig 7).

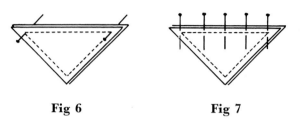

Fig 6   **Fig 7**

6 Starting with a double stitch, sew along the pencilled line with small running stitches about the same length as machine stitches, loading several stitches on to the needle at a time. Begin each run of stitches with a backstitch to secure the work firmly. Finish the seam exactly at the end of the marked line with several backstitches (Fig 8).

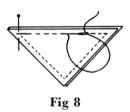

Fig 8

Do not sew into the seam allowances, these are left free so that once the block is complete the seams may be pressed to one side. They are never pressed open, as the hand-sewn stitches are not strong enough. There is no set rule for which way each seam is finally pressed – just press them to avoid too much bulk building up on the back.

7 The squares made from three pieces need to be

SANDRA ROBSON

'My first completed quilt, made in Lynne's class. In my enthusiasm I bought far too many fabrics and found I was always behind everyone as I agonized over what to use for each square. As I'm not an experienced quilter it gave me a real sense of achievement when it was eventually completed. And of course, I have plenty of fabric left over for another quilt!'

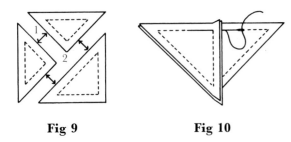

Fig 9   **Fig 10**

sewn in two stages. First join together the two smaller triangles and then sew the halves together to make the square, pinning and matching the seams as before (Fig 9). When sewing this second seam, do not sew over the seam allowances in the middle. Instead, sew up to the seam and make a backstitch. Pass the needle through the seam allowances to the other side. Backstitch again and continue sewing (Fig 10). For the central square sew the triangles into pairs and then join the two halves together (Fig 11).

Once the nine squares are assembled, sew together the horizontal rows of three squares, pinning and matching the seams as before (Fig 12).

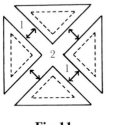
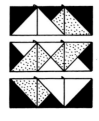

Fig 11   **Fig 12**

8 Join the top two rows by placing them right sides together, matching seams. Push a pin exactly through the seams and corners on each piece. Reposition these pins at right angles to the seams and add more along the seamline, matching the marked lines (Fig 13). Stitch together without sewing over the seam allowances as before. Join on the third row in the same way.

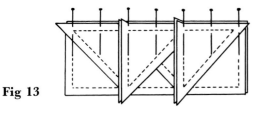

Fig 13

9 If you have chosen to make a larger block, it is now complete, ready for the final sashing strips to be added. If you are making the smaller block it will now need a border. Cut four strips from your chosen fabric, two measuring 2¼ x 9½in (5.7 x 24.2cm) and two measuring 2¼ x 13in (5.7 x 33cm). Using

a sharp marking pencil draw a line on the wrong side of each fabric strip ¼in (6mm) away from one long edge. Mark the line as shown in Fig 14.

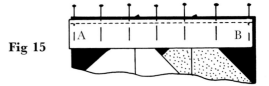

Fig 14

10 With right sides together, pin each shorter strip to opposite sides of the block, matching the marked lines. Marks A and B should match the drawn corners of the block. Use pins as before (Fig 15).

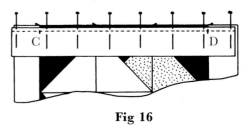

Fig 15

As the block will have been pressed on completion, all the seam allowances will be pressed in the chosen directions. Because of this, these border strips can be stitched on through all the seam allowances if you prefer. Stitch from one end of the strip to the other, not just from A to B. You can stitch these strips on to the block by hand or by machine. Use a machine foot that lets you see the pencilled line as you stitch – a straight stitch foot is ideal – as you need to sew exactly along the drawn line.

Press the two strips outwards. With right sides together, pin the longer strips to the other two sides of the block, matching the marking lines. Marks C and D should be matched with the corners of the block (Fig 16). Stitch along the drawn lines from one end of the strip to the other, not just from C to D. Press the strips outwards.

Fig 16

11 Measure the block, it should be a little more than 12½in (31.7cm) square. Centre it on the cutting board and trim it to an exact 12½in (31.7cm) square, see page 109 for instructions on trimming the blocks.

12 Add the framing sashing strips if you are ready to, see page 110 for instructions.

STRIP RAIL

I first saw this pattern in an American book about quick machined patchwork without templates written by Trudie Hughes, a very clever quilter whose books are always an inspiration and whose techniques are speedy and exciting.

Like Rail Fence the design uses long strips of fabric which are stitched into a band and then cut. Diagonal cutting and stitching creates a strongly diagonal feeling to the block, so it makes a good choice for a corner of your sampler quilt. Very

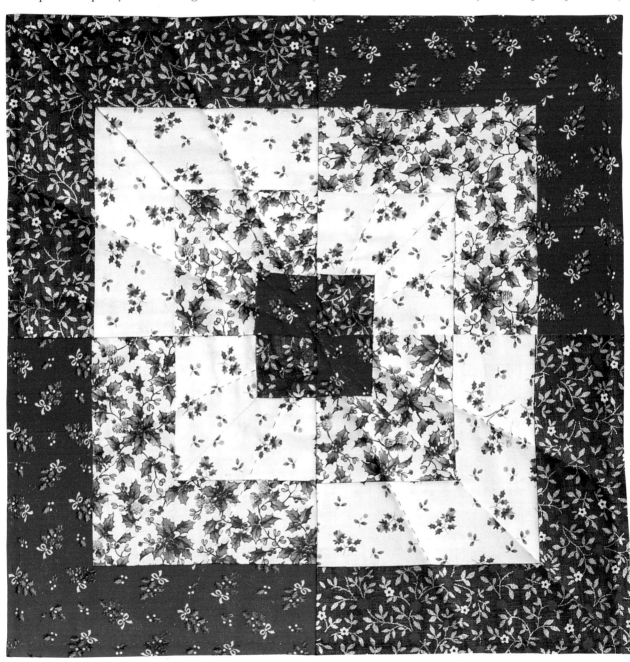

exciting quilt designs can be made from the repeated block, especially if it is placed 'on point' – with the corners of the block at the top, bottom and sides and extra fabric added to make a square (Fig 1). Several

Fig 1

lovely quilt-sized patterns based on Strip Bow (the arrangement shown in Fig 1) can be found in Trudie Hughes' book *Template-free Quiltmaking* published by the American publisher That Patchwork Place.

COLOUR CHOICES

Four fabrics are used in this block and they could be full of contrasts or could graduate in colour from light to dark across the strips. The strongest fabrics are most effective when used on the outside rather than on the inside of the band of four. Take your chosen fabrics and fold them into narrow strips. Place them in order on a flat surface so that you can judge the effect. Rearrange them if necessary until you are happy with the sequence.

CONSTRUCTION

1 From each fabric cut two sets of strips each measuring $2\frac{1}{8}$in (5.3cm) wide and 15in (38cm) long (Fig 2), see page 18 for instructions on cutting strips.

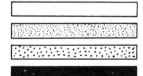

Fig 2

2 Set the stitch length on your sewing machine to about $\frac{2}{3}$ the size of the usual dressmaking stitch to prevent the seams from coming undone when the strips are cut across. As usual, the seams need to be a scant $\frac{1}{4}$in (6mm). Use a strip of masking tape to help you accurately stitch the seams, see page 16 for setting up the machine.

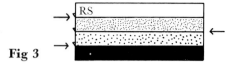

Fig 3

Stitch the four strips together, alternating the direction you sew the strips to keep the band straight and not slightly rippled (Fig 3).

3 Press one band of strips from the *front* with the seams pressed towards the top of the band. Press the second band from the *front* with the seams pressed down towards the bottom of the band (Fig 4). See page 15 for general advice on pressing.

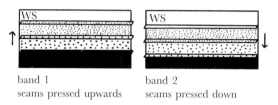

band 1
seams pressed upwards

band 2
seams pressed down

Fig 4

4 Take band one and place it horizontally on the cutting board right side up, lining up the top edge with one of the horizontal markings on the board. If the band is slightly rippled, do not worry, just pat it as flat as you can and carry on. Four different fabrics cannot be expected to lay completely flat when joined. If they do, take all the credit, if they do not, blame the fabric!

Take band two and place it right side down on top of band one, matching colours and seams carefully. The seam allowances go in opposite directions, which helps to line up the seams of the two bands (Fig 5).

5 Measure the width of the bands. If you have stitched an accurate scant $\frac{1}{4}$in (6mm) seam the bands should measure 7in (17.8cm). Using the rotary ruler and cutter, trim one end of the layered bands to straighten them and cut off two sections each 7in (17.8cm) long, to make two layered squares (Fig 6).

NB If your bands do not measure 7in (17.8cm), even if they are only $\frac{1}{8}$in (3mm) out, take the measurement you have and cut the squares to

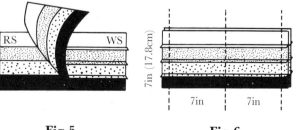

Fig 5 **Fig 6**

MARY TELFORD

*'I chose to make a small sampler quilt using Christmas
fabrics to hang on the wall each December. I was
particularly pleased with the Christmas tree border,
which I sorted out without any help from Teacher.'*

match it. If the two bands are not identical in width it is worth restitching one of them so that they match each other. Always work from the final width measurement of both bands to cut your squares, this way you will finish up with true squares, even if they are slightly more or slightly less than they are supposed to be. You can adjust that later if necessary.

6 Keeping the two layers matching exactly, cut each square diagonally in one direction (Fig 7). Each double layer of triangles is now ready to sew.

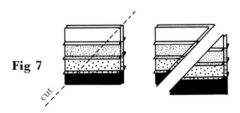

Fig 7

7 Pin the diagonal edges together on all four pairs of triangles, matching the seams. Handle the pieces carefully as the cut edges are on the bias (the diagonal grain of the fabric) and will be very stretchy. This stretchiness can be a help, though, if you are having to do a bit of easing to make the seams match. Machine-stitch along each diagonal seam. Press from the front of the work, pressing the seam allowances to one side. The resulting four squares show two different colour arrangements (Fig 8).

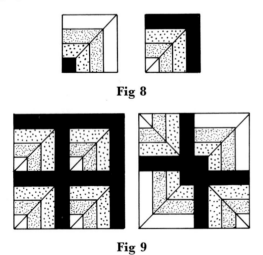

Fig 8

Fig 9

8 Arrange the four squares until you find a design you like, two alternatives are shown in Fig 9, although more are possible, so keep moving the squares around until you find your favourite.

9 Pin and machine-stitch the top two squares together with a ¼in (6mm) seam. If you place the pins at right angles to the seams you will be able to

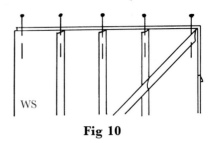

WS

Fig 10

stitch right up to each pin before you need to remove it (Fig 10).

If the two edges do not match exactly and one is shorter than the other, pin and stitch with the shorter edge on top, as this will stretch slightly as you stitch and should ease the problem. Press the seams to one side from the front of the joined squares.

10 Pin and machine-stitch the second pair of squares. Press the seams in the opposite direction to the first half (Fig 11).

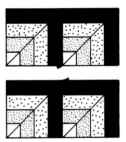

Fig 11

11 Join the two halves by stitching across with a ¼in (6mm) seam, taking care to match the centre seams. Pressing the centre seams of each half in opposite directions will help you to match them accurately, as they lock into each other as you sew. Pin diagonally as this helps to keep both sets of seam allowances flat while stitching (Fig 12). The final long seam can be pressed to one side or, if this makes it too bulky, press the seam open.

Fig 12

12 The finished block should measure slightly more than 12½in (31.7cm) square. If this is the case, centre it on a cutting board and trim it down to an exact 12½in (31.7cm) square. See page 109 for instructions on trimming the blocks. Add the framing sashing strips, following the instructions on page 110.

CURVED SEAM PATCHWORK

DRUNKARD'S PATH

This design originated in England where it was known as Robbing Peter to Pay Paul. It travelled to America with the early settlers who gradually developed a whole series of designs based on sixteen squares, each of which is divided into two parts, a quadrant (quarter circle) and the remainder of the square (Fig 1). As the block patterns evolved they were given a variety of names: Wanderer in the Wilderness, Solomon's Puzzle, Old Maid's Puzzle and the most well known Drunkard's Path.

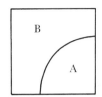

Fig 1

The arrangement of the sixteen squares, four in each of four rows, changes the block design so much that it is quite possible to include several Drunkard's Path blocks in a sampler quilt without anyone realizing that they are the same basic design; Fig 2 shows six different arrangements, each using just two fabrics. This block is another that is constructed by American piecing, with the new problem of sewing the curved seam that joins shapes A and B to make a square. There are sixteen of these seams in the block, so by the time you have finished you should have become quite used to it! This traditional curved seam block and its many variations is a great favourite of mine.

COLOUR CHOICES

The designs in Fig 2 use two fabrics only, although you might like to use more, as shown in Fig 3. As you have now made quite a number of blocks, it is

Fig 3

always a good idea to lay them all out while you choose the fabric for this design. If there is one fabric that seems to jar you must decide whether it was a mistake or whether you just need to use more of it in future blocks. Assemble your fabrics according to which arrangement of Drunkard's Path you have chosen and decide which fabric is to go where in the design. You may find it easier to make a rough sketch or tracing of the block and colour it in so that you know how many of each shape you need to cut out from each fabric.

CONSTRUCTION

1 Make card templates by tracing templates A and B from Fig 4 and cutting them out. These are combined to make a 3in (7.6cm) square, sixteen squares will make the block. Stick the traced shapes on to card, or use template plastic, see page 15 for instructions on making templates.

2 Use your coloured drawing of the block to check how many of each template shape you need in

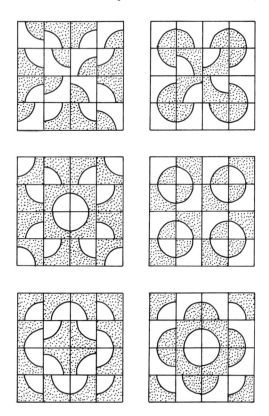

Fig 2

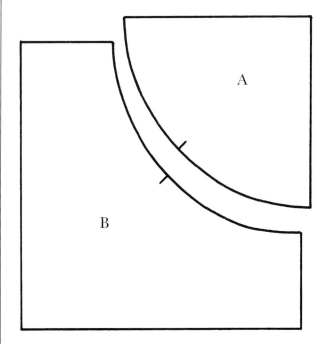

Fig 4 Templates – actual size

each fabric. For instance, for the Drunkard's Path block shown first in Fig 2 you need eight of template A and eight of template B from each of the two fabrics.

3 On the wrong side of each fabric draw accurately around the templates using a sharp marking pencil. This marks the sewing line. Mark the centre point on each curve in the seam allowance (Fig 5). Allow at least ½in (1.2cm)

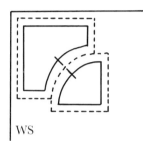

Fig 5   WS

between each drawn outline so that a seam allowance of ¼in (6mm) can be added to each shape when cutting out. Save space by arranging the shapes on the fabric as shown in Fig 6.

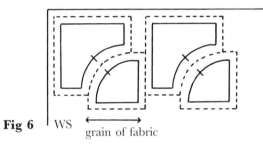

Fig 6   WS
grain of fabric

4 Cut out each shape to include the ¼in (6mm) seam allowance, do this either by eye or by using a quilter's quarter, a seamwheel or a small rotary cutter with a seam guide attachment, see Basic Equipment page 10.

5 Arrange the cut pieces on a flat surface or pin them in position on a polystyrene tile or board. You may find that you rearrange the pieces to make a completely new design. Always keep an open and flexible attitude as you work and be prepared to change your mind if you come up with a better alternative.

6 Take the two shapes A and B which make up one of the sixteen squares in the design. Using a small pair of scissors with sharp points, clip the curved seam alllowance on shape B, snipping at roughly ¼in (6mm) intervals, going nearly but not quite to the drawn line (Fig 7).

7 Joining shape A to shape B seems straightforward when the pieces are arranged in the block, but they do not seem to match at all

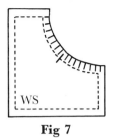

Fig 7

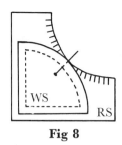

Fig 8

when you place them right sides together ready for pinning. The only way you can make them fit each other is by curving the pieces in your hand as you pin, like setting in a sleeve in dressmaking.

Match the centre marks on each piece by pushing a pin through both layers of fabric until the head is on the surface of the top fabric. Reposition the pin at right angles to the seam. I find it easier to sew if I arrange the pins with the points outwards, that way I don't bleed all over the fabric (Fig 8). Swing one corner of shape A round to match the corner of shape B, lining up the straight outer edges of both pieces. Align the corners of the sewing lines by pushing through a pin (Fig 9). Swing the other corner of shape A

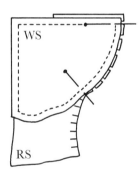

Fig 9

round and match and pin the drawn corners, aligning the two straight edges. The resultant shape cannot be held flat – it takes on a deep curve as in Fig 10. More pins are needed to fix one drawn line exactly on top of the other, so match and pin the

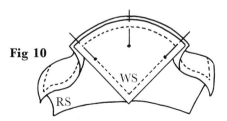

Fig 10

two pieces at intervals no greater than ½in (1.2cm), closer if you need to. This makes a real hedgehog of a seam, bristling with pins, but it is the only way to keep the lines matching exactly (Fig 11).

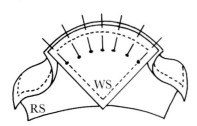

Fig 11

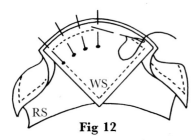

Fig 12

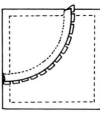

Fig 14

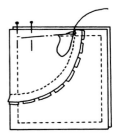

Fig 15

8 Sew along the pencilled line with small running stitches removing the pins as you go, see Maple Leaf page 31 for more detailed instructions. Do not sew into the seam allowances at either end of the curve (Fig 12).

You may find it easier to pin the curve with shape B on the top so that the seam curves away from you. Alternatively you may find it easier to ease in the fullness by curving it over your hand while you pin and sew (Fig 13). Try both ways and see which you prefer.

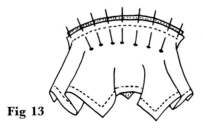

Fig 13

9 Press the completed square from the front with the curved seam towards the larger shape B. This way the clipped edges spread and help reduce the bulk of the seam so that it lies flat (Fig 14).
10 Assemble each of the sixteen squares in this way, then arrange them into your chosen design. Join the squares into horizontal rows, pinning and matching the seams in the usual way. Join the rows together to complete the block. Just this once I break the rule of not sewing across the seam allowances when stitching across the curved seam as it has already been pressed to one side (Fig 14). I sew from one marked corner of the square to the other, sewing right across the pressed curved seam allowances (Fig 15).

It is quite possible to assemble the squares of this block by machine if you prefer. Pin the two squares together, matching the drawn lines in the same way as for hand piecing. Machine-stitch carefully along the drawn line using a straight stitch foot so that you can see exactly where you are stitching. It is usual when machine-stitching the marked lines to sew beyond the drawn lines into the seam allowances, right across the fabric from edge to edge.

Join each row of four squares. Press from the front, ironing the seams of row one in one direction, those in row two the opposite way and so on, as in the Trip Around The World block page 36. When you join the rows together, match and pin the drawn lines carefully and machine-stitch along the drawn line right across the fabric, stitching through all the seam allowances.

NB Do not attempt to machine the curved seam itself on this 3in (7.6cm) square, you are likely to trap tiny pleats in the seam as you sew.
11 Press the completed block from the front and measure it, it should be 12½in (31.7cm) square. If it is not, make adjustments to bring it to the exact size by trimming or adding a narrow border, see page 109 for instructions on trimming and bordering blocks.
12 Add the framing sashing strips, following the instructions on page 110.

DOT SIDGWICK

'My quilt was built around the colours in the flowery border. Originally I only wanted to use pale greens and pinks, but it looked rather dull when I started to add green borders. I then changed to black and the whole quilt seemed to sharpen up, making the very light green and deep pink look much more vibrant!'

MACHINED STRIP PATCHWORK

SPIDER'S WEB

This kaleidoscopic design used to be painstakingly hand-pieced, using templates to get all the little strips. With rotary cutters and quick piecing techniques it has become another one of those clever join-the-strips-cut-it-up-again processes. It looks won-derful when all eight segments have been joined to form the final design, so that the eight points all meet in the centre. Many patchwork designs have six or eight corners meeting and they do not always work out as well as the maker hopes. The trick is to get it

right at each stage of construction so that mistakes are corrected as you go along rather than finishing up with a jumble of points and angles at the end and with no idea how to correct them.

COLOUR CHOICES

Four fabrics are used in a sequence of strips, so look at the blocks you have already completed to see which fabrics could be reintroduced. You may already have a block which uses four fabrics that you could use again. The fabrics are joined to form a long band, which is then cut and turned in alternate directions, so that the top and bottom colours come together to form the centre and the two middle colours alternate with each other in the design (Fig 1). Cut out the corner triangles when the web has been made as it will be much easier to choose the fabric which looks best then.

Fig 1

CONSTRUCTION

1 Make templates A and B from Fig 2 page 56 in the usual way, see page 15 for instructions on making templates. Mark the three dotted lines and the three dots on template A. Push a large pin through each dot on template A to make a hole, it needs to be big enough to take the point of a pencil so you can mark fabric through it.

2 Cut a strip 2 x 30in (5 x 76cm) from each of your four chosen fabrics.

3 Machine-stitch the strips together with the usual small stitch and a ¼in (6mm) seam allowance. Remember to alternate the direction you sew the strips as explained in Rail Fence page 27. Press the band from the front with the seams all in one direction (Fig 3).

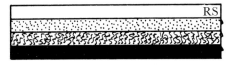

Fig 3

4 Place the fabric band on a cutting board wrong side up. Place template A on the band, it should fit exactly from top to bottom with the stitched seams matching the dotted lines on the template (Fig 4). If it does not, it is worth restitching the seams to get a good fit. It is important that the template fits properly top to bottom, if the seamlines do not match the dotted lines on the template, do not worry too much.

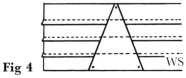

Fig 4

Using a sharp pencil, draw down both sides of the template and mark the dots. Move the template along the band, turning it through 180° to fit against the first drawn shape, now draw round the template again. Continue this way until eight shapes have been marked on the band (Fig 5). If two

Fig 5

shapes do not fit against each other accurately, leave a small space between them if necessary – the band is long enough to allow you to do this (Fig 6). Mark the dots on each shape.

5 Use a rotary cutter and ruler to cut the drawn lines. Now arrange the eight triangular shapes to make a spider's web.

6 First join the triangles in pairs, matching the seams carefully and stitching right through the marked dots on both pieces (Fig 7). Take care that

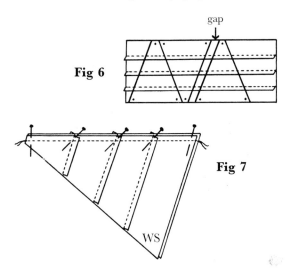

Fig 6

Fig 7

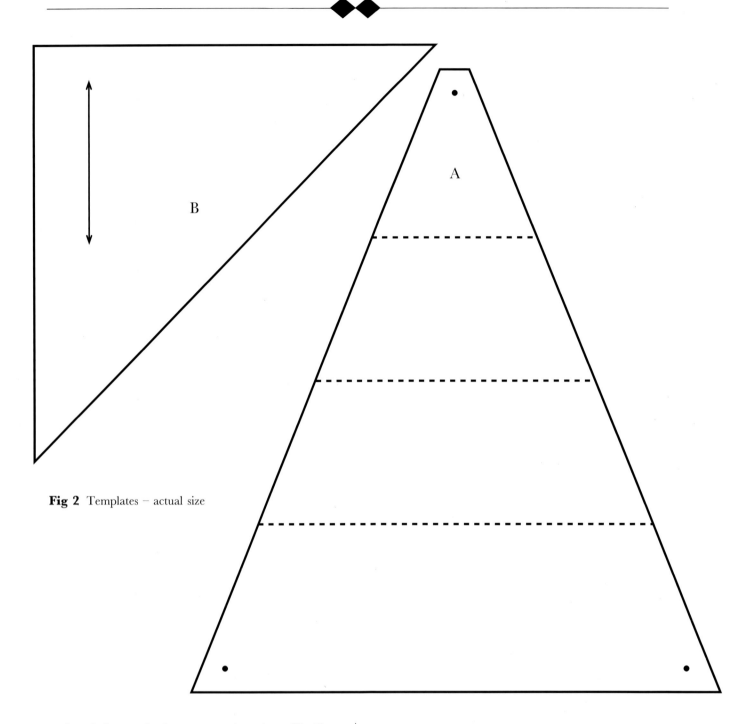

Fig 2 Templates – actual size

each pair is exactly the same as the others (Fig 8) and not stitched together in the reverse order (Fig 9) otherwise they will not fit together to make the design. Press the seams from the front to one side.

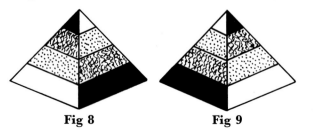

Fig 8   **Fig 9**

ANN LARKIN

'The selection of rich brown fabrics used in this quilt were chosen deliberately to complement the fitted wardrobes and cupboards surrounding the bed. Golds, beiges and greens were added and the quilt finished with a Drunkard's Path border.'

7 Now pin two pieces together matching dots carefully and stitch through them as accurately as possible. Do not have your machine-stitch length set too small in case you need to unpick the stitches at some stage. Repeat this process with the other two pieces. Now comes quality control time. Open out each half and inspect them from the front. You are aiming to have the two inner fabrics meeting in an arrowhead exactly ¼in (6mm) away from the top edges of the fabrics (Fig 10).

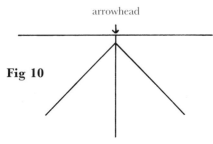

Fig 10

If you have successfully matched the arrowheads, but it is less than ¼in (6mm) from the top edges, resew the centre seam (the last one to have been sewn), stitching just inside the original stitches – there is no need to unpick these stitches as they are now in the seam allowance. However, if the arrowheads are *not* matching but look like Fig 11, unpick the centre seam, match the dots more carefully and stitch again. If you take time to get the two halves of the web right at this stage they will match more accurately in the final long seam.

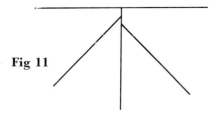

Fig 11

When you are happy with the arrowheads, press from the front, pressing the seams to one side.

8 Pin the two halves together, matching the seams along the edges and taking care to position the tips of the two arrowheads in the centre exactly on top of each other. Check by peeling the top half back with the pin. When the arrowheads match, hold them in position firmly and pin on both sides of the centre seam. I use extra-long, extra-fine pins so that I can machine-stitch over them if necessary (Fig 12). Stitch the seam.

Now check from the front. If you have lost the tips of the arrowheads your seam allowance was too wide. Finger press the seam open and check

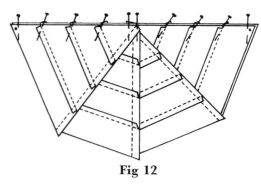

Fig 12

how the centre looks – this can make quite a difference to the balance of the central eight points. If you are unhappy with the result, unpick 2in (5cm) or so either side of the centre and try again. Do the best you can and remember that only you will notice if it is not perfect. Finally press the long seam open from the back of the work.

9 The large triangles from template B form the four corners of the block. They can be placed adjacent to the sides or edges that use fabric one or adjacent to the sides using fabric four (Fig 13), so choose the fabric that works best for these corners.

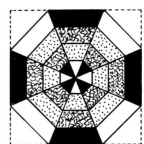

Fig 13

Draw round the template on the wrong side of the chosen fabric four times and cut out exactly on the line as no extra seam allowance is needed.

10 With right sides together, pin and stitch each corner to the block, matching the long edge of shape B with the outer edge of the block (Fig 14).

11 Press the corners with the seams outwards. Trim the block to an exact 12½in (31.7cm) square, see page 109 for instructions on trimming the blocks. Add the framing sashing strips, see page 110 for instructions.

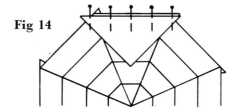

Fig 14

GRANDMOTHER'S FAN

This traditional block has always been pieced by hand, but nearly all of it can be easily machine-pieced if you prefer. It features the curving lines used in Drunkard's Path, but on a larger scale to give a fan shape. The fan is divided into six sections, although in old quilts it can often be seen with up to ten divisions. Compared with piecing the Drunkard's Path curves this one is really quick and easy. There are only two curves to be pieced and one of them is so large that it hardly seems like a curve at all.

The centre of Grandmother's Fan is not in the middle of the block but in the corner, which makes it an ideal design to use in a corner of the sampler quilt where it gives weight and encourages the eye to move inwards to the rest of the quilt. This simple block has been repeated and combined to make the beautiful blue and white quilt in the project on page 139.

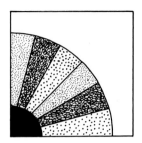

Fig 1

COLOUR CHOICES

The fan has six segments which can be made from six different fabrics or, as shown in Fig 1, from three fabrics repeated in sequence. A striking design can also be made with just two contrasting fabrics used alternately in the segments. The background is quite a large, empty area of fabric, so if you choose a plain fabric you may need to break it up visually with quilting. The central quadrant is like the eye of a flower and should be strong enough to give the fan a focus without dominating everything else. If you are not sure which centre or background fabrics will look best, cut and piece together the fan before making a decision.

CONSTRUCTION

1 Make templates A and B from Fig 2 in the usual way, see page 15 for instructions on making templates. The background shape is too large for a template to be given here, so make it in the following way.

On a large piece of graph paper draw a 12in (30.5cm) square. Set a pair of compasses at a distance of 10in (25.4cm). I use an extra long pencil in the compasses. Fix the point of the compasses in a corner of the drawn square and draw a quadrant as shown in Fig 3. The shaded section of the square will be your template. If you cannot make your compasses reach to 10in

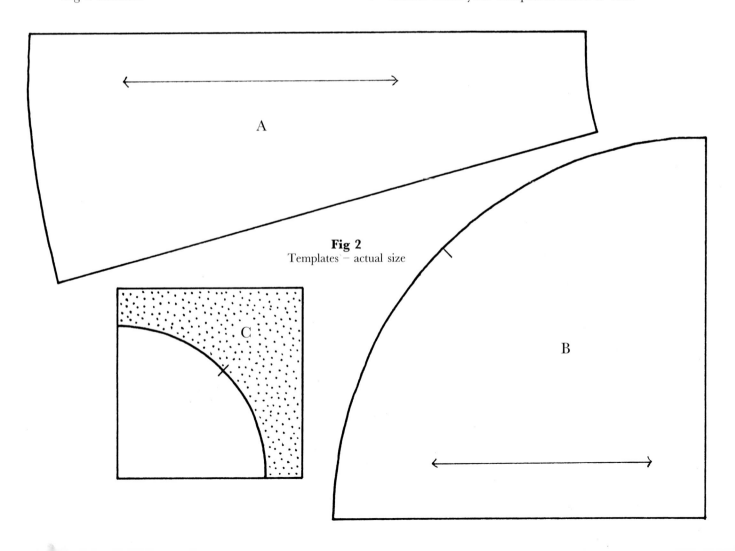

Fig 2
Templates – actual size

KATE KEARNEY

*'My principal feeling about this quilt is that if I could
do it, then anyone could! It was very difficult to find
enough fabrics in the colours I wanted. On reflection,
this restriction has made the quilt more harmonious.'*

61

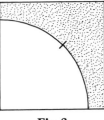

Fig 3

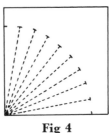

Fig 4

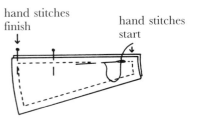

hand stitches finish

hand stitches start

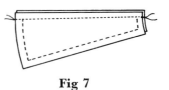

machine-stitch across seam allowance

Fig 7

(25.4cm) use a ruler and mark 10in (25.4cm) at roughly ½in (1.2cm) intervals. Join these marks by eye to make the curve (Fig 4). Mark the centre of the curve by placing a ruler diagonally across two corners of the square and marking the point where the ruler crosses the curve. Stick the template on to card as usual.

2 On the wrong side of your chosen fabrics draw accurately around the fan template A using a sharp marking pencil. This marks the sewing line. Allow at least ½in (1.2cm) between each drawn outline so that a seam allowance of ¼in (6mm) can be added to each shape when cutting out (Fig 5). You need six shape A pieces. You also need one shape B and one shape C.

3 Cut out each shape to include the ¼in (6mm) seam allowance, judging this by eye or using a quilter's quarter, a seamwheel or small rotary cutter with a seam guide attachment, see Basic Equipment page 10.

4 Arrange the segments of the fan on a flat surface or pin them in position on a polystyrene tile or board. Move them around to check that you like the sequence of fabrics. At the same time see how effective your chosen centre and background fabrics are. There is still time to make changes before joining everything together.

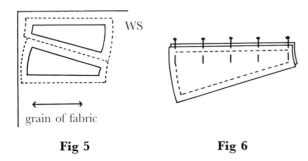

WS

grain of fabric

Fig 5

Fig 6

5 Take the first two segments of shape A and place them right sides together, matching the drawn lines with pins (Fig 6) as in the Maple Leaf block page 31. Stitch along the drawn lines either by hand or machine. If by hand, sew along the lines but not into the seam allowances at either end. If by machine, stitch along the lines from one

end of the fabric to the other including the seam allowances (Fig 7). Join all six pieces of the fan together in this way. Press the seams from the front of the work to one side.

6 Clip the seam allowance of the fan along the smaller curved edge (Fig 8). Pin and sew the fan to the centre piece B in the same way as described for Drunkard's Path. I am quite happy sewing this by hand, but do try it by machine if you want to. Press the seam towards the fan, pressing from the front as usual.

7 Clip the seam allowance of the curved edge of the large background piece. Pin the longer curve of the fan to the clipped edge of the background, matching corners and centres carefully (Fig 9), as described in Drunkard's Path page 49. Press the seam towards the background fabric.

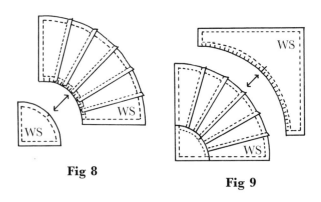

WS

WS

WS

WS

Fig 8

Fig 9

8 Measure the completed block, it should be 12½in (31.7cm) square. If it needs trimming, trim away from the two sides of the background fabric *only*, leaving the fan its full size, see page 109 for instructions on trimming the blocks.

9 Add the framing sashing strips, see page 110 for instructions.

QUICK MACHINED STRIP PATCHWORK

LOG CABIN

Log Cabin quilts have been part of the European quilt heritage for several hundred years. The design appears in Dutch, Swedish and British quilts of the nineteenth century and earlier and it is likely that settlers took it to America where it has become one of the most popular of the traditional quilt patterns.

The design is made of rectangular strips of light and dark fabrics arranged around a central square. Traditionally the strips represented the wooden logs that made up the pioneer's log cabin. The central

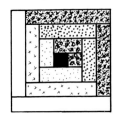

Fig 1

square was either red to represent the fire in the hearth or yellow for the welcoming light in the window. Light and dark scraps of fabric were cut into strips of the correct length using templates, and then pieced together around the centres to make squares which showed strongly contrasting areas of light and dark (Fig 1).

This is still the way the design is worked today, but modern cutting and stitching techniques have revolutionized the speed and accuracy with which a quilt can be assembled. In the sampler quilt four identical squares of Log Cabin are made at the same time in a mass production method. These are then joined together to make the final block.

COLOUR CHOICES

Choosing fabric for Log Cabin is always tortuous. You need two sets of fabric showing a distinct difference from each other – a dark set contrasting with a light set or a set of plain shades against patterned, or even a complete change of colour like red fabrics against black. Within these sets the fabrics should be similar so that they blend together without one standing out against the others too much. Lay your fabrics out on a flat surface, overlapping so that you get an idea what ³/₄in (1.9cm) strips will look like when stitched together. Arrange them in the two sets and avoid using a fabric that does not obviously belong in either set. For instance if you are using dark green fabrics with light cream fabrics do not include a medium green and cream print which could be part of either set. You will lose the element of contrast that gives the block its distinctive appearance. If you have a limited number of fabrics to choose from you could restrict them to two fabrics in each set and use them alternately as in Fig 2. The central square does not have to be the traditional red

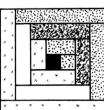

Fig 2

or yellow, it can be anything you like. In the Log Cabin cot quilt project on page 128 I have used yellow fabrics for one set and blues for the other with blue centres. You may prefer a strong spot of colour for each centre or a colour that does not match either set of strips but gently complements them. Study some of the Log Cabin blocks in the sampler quilts shown in this book and choose whichever effect you like best.

CONSTRUCTION

1 Cut strips 1¹/₄in (3.2cm) wide from each fabric and arrange them at the side of the sewing machine in the order they will be used. A total length of about 10ft (3m) of strips for each set is needed.

2 Cut a short strip about 7in (17.8cm) long and 1¹/₄in (3.2cm) wide from the centre fabric. Cut pieces from this strip to give four 1¹/₄in (3.2cm) squares (Fig 3).

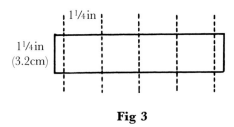

Fig 3

3 Stick a small square of masking tape on to the back of one of these central squares, avoiding the ¹/₄in (6mm) seam allowance. Label the tape with numbers 1, 2, 3 and 4, as shown in Fig 4. The numbers give a guide to where each strip will be stitched.

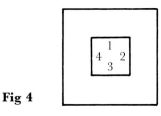

Fig 4

4 Choose the fabric you wish to use first and place it right side *up* on the machine in the correct position for a ¹/₄in (6mm) seam to be sewn. Lower the pressure foot and wind the needle down into the fabric. Now the pressure foot can be lifted and the central squares added without the first strip slipping out of position.

5 Place the first square right side *down* on the strip with side one on the masking tape as the edge to be stitched. Using a short stitch and a ¼in (6mm) seam, sew the central square on to the strip. Sew onwards a few stitches and place a second square right side *down* on the strip. Sew this square in position then add the third and fourth squares in the same way (Fig 5).

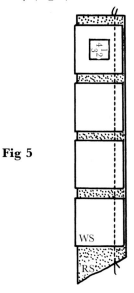

Fig 5

6 Remove the strip from the machine and carefully trim it to match the central squares exactly, using either sharp scissors or a rotary cutter (Fig 6). Finger press the seams away from the squares by holding the central square between your finger and thumb and pushing the strip away from the centre with your thumbs, pressing the seam firmly (Fig 7).

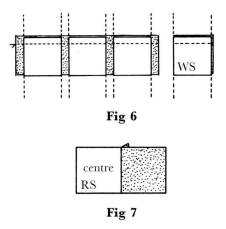

Fig 6

Fig 7

7 In building up the Log Cabin rounds of strips surrounding the centre, each fabric is always used twice, making an L-shape. So put the same fabric strip on the sewing machine again, right side *up* and wind the needle down into the fabric. Take the original block with its piece of masking tape and place it right side *down* on the strip with side

two at the edge to be sewn (Fig 8). Sew down this edge and place the second block on the strip in the same way. The first block is your model and the next three blocks must follow the same arrangement as they are positioned on the strip. Sew down and add the third and fourth blocks to match (Fig 9).

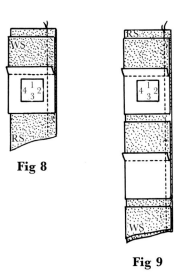

Fig 8

Fig 9

Trim the strip to match exactly the edges of the four blocks (Fig 10). Finger press the seams away from the centre square (Fig 11).

8 Having sewn on two strips from the first fabric, take a strip of fabric from the contrasting set and fix it under the machine, right side *up* with the needle wound down into it. If you were using dark fabrics, now change to light, or go from plain to patterned. Position the original block with side three on the masking tape at the sewing edge (Fig 12). Sew down

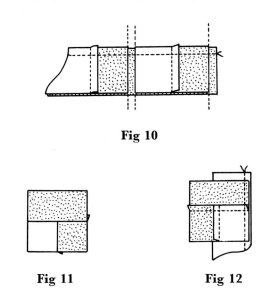

Fig 10

Fig 11   **Fig 12**

this edge and add the remaining three blocks to match the first (Fig 13). Trim the strips to match each block and finger press the seams away from the centre (Fig 14).

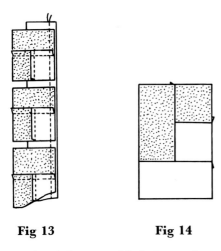

Fig 13   **Fig 14**

9 Using a strip of the same fabric (remember, always use each fabric *twice* to make an L-shape), follow the same procedure, sewing the strip on to side four. You now have a complete round of strips surrounding the central square (Fig 15).

Now you have completed this much there is a quick way to see at a glance which side is the next to be stitched. Look at the block and find the edge which has two seams along it. This is the side which is to be stitched next (Fig 16).

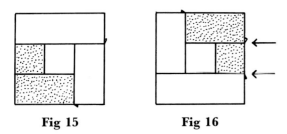

Fig 15   **Fig 16**

10 Continue building up the design, referring to the masking tape square. Sides one and two always have the same set of fabrics against them and sides three and four always have the contrasting set of fabrics. Remember to use each fabric *twice* to make the L-shape.

The sequence of fabrics is: two sides from first fabric from set one, two sides from first fabric from set two, two sides from second fabric from set one, two sides from second fabric from set two and so on.

11 When three rounds of strips have been sewn, check against Fig 1 that you have attached the correct number of strips and press each square from the front.

12 Arrange the four squares in the design you like best. Pin and machine-stitch the top two squares together with a $\frac{1}{4}$in (6mm) seam as usual. If the two edges do not match exactly and one is shorter than the other, pin and stitch with the shorter edge on top as this will stretch slightly as you work and should ease the problem. Press the seam from the front to one side.

13 Pin and stitch the second pair of squares, pressing the centre seams in the opposite direction to the first half (Fig 17).

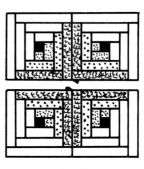

Fig 17

14 Join the two halves, matching the centre seams carefully. The final long seam can be pressed to one side, or if this makes it too bulky, press the seam allowances open.

15 Measure the completed block, it should be about 11in (28cm) square. Choose a fabric to use as an extra frame around the block before the sashing. Cut strips $1\frac{1}{2}$in (3.8cm) wide for this frame and attach them, see page 109 for instructions on trimming and adding frames.

Trim the block to an exact $12\frac{1}{2}$in (31.7cm) square. Add the framing sashing strips, see page 110, for instructions.

JANE HODGES

'My sampler quilt was my first attempt at patchwork. The choice of colours is a reflection of my upbringing in the southern hemisphere, and the quilt became affectionately known as "Have you seen that blue and yellow thing round the corner?".'

QUICK MACHINED STRIP PATCHWORK

COURTHOUSE STEPS

This is a variation of Log Cabin and can be used for another block in the sampler quilt as it looks very different. The fabrics are the same as for Log Cabin, but they are used to create a more symmetrical design in each block (Fig 1).

CONSTRUCTION

1 Proceed exactly as for Log Cabin, cutting similar strips and centres.
2 Add the first fabric twice, but at *opposite* sides of the central square (sides one and three marked on the masking tape) (Fig 2). The first contrasting fabric is then sewn on to sides two and four (Fig 3).
3 Continue to add strips, the first set of fabrics

going on sides one and three, the contrasting set on sides two and four, until three rounds have been attached.
4 Join the squares together and add a frame and sashing as for Log Cabin.

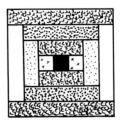

Fig 1   **Fig 2**   **Fig 3**

HELEN BURRETT

*'Just six fabrics were used to produce this sampler
quilt. Decisions were quickly reached when choosing
fabrics for each block, but it was also necessary
to take care that neither green nor pink became the
dominant colour.'*

Pieced Patchwork

—

Dresden Plate

There are many patchwork blocks based on the circular plate design and Dresden Plate is the most popular and well known of these. The number of segments in the plate varies from eight to twenty, while the outer edges may be all curved, all pointed or a mixture of the two. No particular number or layout is obligatory, so it can be varied at the whim of the maker. Here the Dresden Plate has twelve sections, four with pointed edges to give a stronger accent at the top, bottom and two sides (Fig 1). The

Fig 1

segments are joined to make the plate, which is then appliquéd on to a background. The outer edges have to be turned over and tacked before being stitched to the background. Finally the central circle is appliquéd in position. So this block is as much about appliqué as it is about piecing.

COLOUR CHOICES

This is another block, like Grandmother's Fan and Tumbling Blocks, that has a design set on a background, so when choosing the fabrics arrange them on the background fabric to get an idea of how they look. You may be varying your backgrounds or keeping them all one colour, but you need to pin up or lay out all the completed blocks to check how the selection and balance of colours is going. If it is not

possible to pin them on to a vertical surface, lay them on the floor and view them from as great a distance as possible – stand on a chair or even a step-ladder. Note the fabrics you need to use more of and what is needed to keep a good balance. You will be surprised at how much easier this gets as you complete more blocks.

For the segments choose a selection of three fabrics that are equal in tone. Try to avoid one that is much stronger than the others or use it for the pointed-edged segments to make a cross. You can leave the decision about the central circle until later if you are not sure what to use at this stage.

CONSTRUCTION

1 Make templates A, B and C from Fig 2 in the usual way, see page 15 for instructions on making templates.
2 On the wrong side of your chosen fabrics draw accurately around template A and template B using a sharp marking pencil. You need eight A shapes and four B shapes. Mark the lines X in the seam allowances on each piece (Fig 3). Allow at least ½in (1.2cm) between each drawn outline so that a seam allowance of ¼in (6mm) can be added to each shape when cutting out. Save space by arranging the shapes as in Fig 4.

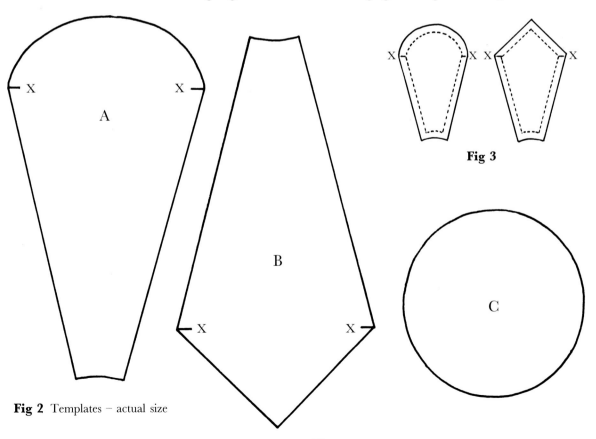

Fig 3

Fig 2 Templates – actual size

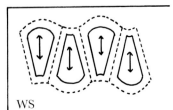

Fig 4   WS

3 Cut out each shape to include the ¼in (6mm) seam allowance, judging this by eye or by using a quilter's quarter, seamwheel or small rotary cutter with a seam guide attachment, see Basic Equipment page 10.

4 Arrange the segments on the background fabric to check that you are happy with the sequence of fabrics before stitching them together.

5 Take two adjacent segments and place them right sides together, matching the drawn lines with pins from the corner to the lines marked X (Fig 5),

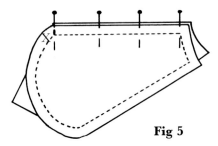

Fig 5

as in Maple Leaf page 31. Stitch along the drawn lines either by hand or machine, beginning and finishing at the corner of the design and at X (Fig 6). Join all twelve segments together in this way to make a complete circle (Fig 7). Press the seams from the front of the work to one side.

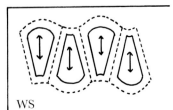

Fig 6

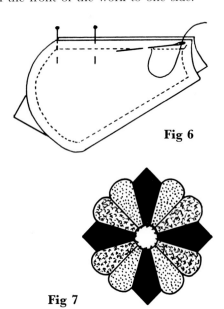

Fig 7

6 Turn the 'plate' to the wrong side and carefully clip the seam allowance of the curved outer edge, snipping at roughly ¼in (6mm) intervals, going nearly but not quite to the drawn line. The seam allowances along the outer edge of the 'plate' need to be turned to the back of the work and tacked. The turning lines are most easily marked by the traditional technique called needle-marking.

Lay the 'plate' right side down on a pad of folded fabric (a folded flannelette sheet is ideal). Position template A on one of the curved segments exactly on the drawn outline. Using a large blunt tapestry needle, trace around the curved edge of the template, holding the needle at an angle and pressing firmly. You should find that the needle has pressed a crease along the drawn curved line (Fig 8).

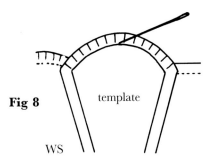

Fig 8   template

WS

Repeat this on all eight curved edges, then use template B to needle-mark the pointed edges of the remaining four segments.

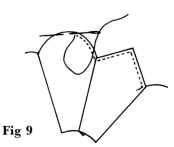

Fig 9

7 Turn over the 'plate' to its front and, following the creased lines, turn under the outer edges to the back of the work, tacking them down with small running stitches as you go (Fig 9). Do not press this tacked edge. It will be easier to appliqué the 'plate' on to the background in a really smooth curve if the edge is unpressed so that any little irregularities along it can be adjusted as it is stitched.

8 Cut a 13in (33cm) square of fabric for the background. This allows for any pulling in of the background when the 'plate' is appliquéd on to it and can be trimmed to the exact size later on.

Fold the background square of fabric into quarters and press lightly to mark the centre.

CHRIS WASE

*'The blocks for my quilt were made during evening classes
and the rest on occasional weekend classes.
The border was chosen to complement the quilt and because
it would be quick. In fact, it led to more and more quilting
which took longer than the rest of the quilt!'*

73

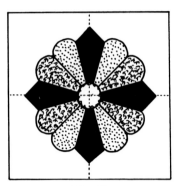

Fig 10

Unfold it and position on the 'plate', centering the creased lines within the hole in the plate (Fig 10). Pin or tack the 'plate' on to the background and, using thread to match the fabrics of it and not the background, sew the 'plate' in position using small, even slip stitches (Fig 11). Sew a double stitch at each inner corner to secure it. Press from the front.

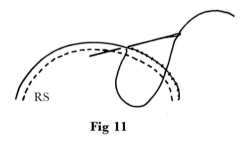

RS

Fig 11

9 On the wrong side of your chosen fabric draw around circle template C and cut it out with a ¼in (6mm) seam allowance added. Make a line of small tacking stitches close to the outer edge of the fabric circle (Fig 12a). Place the card template on the wrong side of the fabric and pull the tacking stitches so that the edges of the fabric are gathered tightly over the card (Fig 12b). Secure with a double stitch and press lightly from the front. Remove the card circle by bending it slightly. Pin the fabric on to the centre of the 'plate' and stitch in place.

Alternatively you might like to try freezer paper to make the circle in this design, see Basic

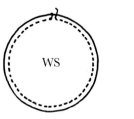

WS

Fig 12a

card circle

Fig 12b

Equipment page 10. On the freezer paper draw round template C and cut it out exactly. Iron the circle, shiny side down, on to the wrong side of the fabric. Cut around it with a ¼in (6mm) seam allowance. Clip the curve nearly but not quite to the freezer paper (Fig 13a). Carefully peel off the circle, replacing it in exactly the same position but with the shiny side facing upwards (Fig 13b). Using the tip of an iron, push the seam allowance over the freezer paper, sticking it down as you go. Take care not to press in any tiny pleats on the outer edge but keep the curve smooth (Fig 13c). If there are areas you are not happy with, just peel the fabric back and repress in the correct position. Place the circle of fabric in the centre of the 'plate' and press. This will fix it on to the background while you stitch it in place.

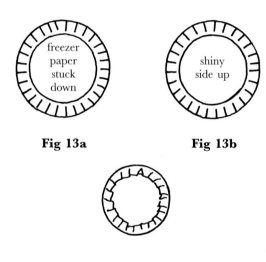

freezer paper stuck down

shiny side up

Fig 13a   **Fig 13b**

Fig 13b

10 If you use freezer paper, cut away the background fabric after the block has been completed to remove the paper and reduce the layers for quilting. If the centre has been appliquéd in the normal way it is up to you whether you cut the background away, although it does allow the block to lie flatter and will be easier to quilt, see Tumbling Blocks page 22 for instructions on cutting away the background.
11 Trim the block to an exact 12½in (31.7cm) square, see page 109 for instructions on trimming the blocks.
12 Add the framing sashing strips, see page 110 for instructions.

TRIANGLES

Patchwork designs worked by the early American pioneers depended greatly on the simple square, as it provided a way of making a quilt from scraps quickly and with little wastage. Large squares were often combined with groups of four smaller squares in a checker-board arrangement to create more elaborate designs and as a way of using up scraps.

An exciting progression from these squares was to divide the square diagonally into two right-angled triangles (Fig 1). These triangles were combined with

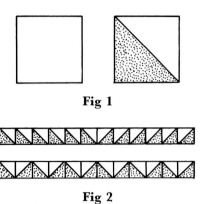

Fig 1

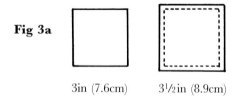

Fig 2

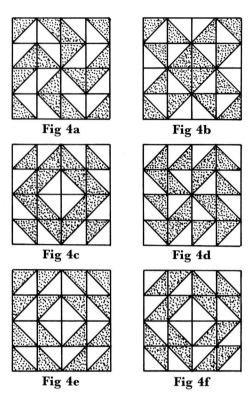

Fig 4a	**Fig 4b**
Fig 4c	**Fig 4d**
Fig 4e	**Fig 4f**

squares and other triangles to create a huge number of block patterns, as well as decorative borders and edgings (Fig 2). The usual method of making these designs was to make a template, cut out the shapes, then piece them together by hand or machine, following the drawn sewing lines in the American piecing technique. However, there is a quicker and easier way of turning the triangles into squares by using rotary equipment and a sewing machine. You still have the tiresome task of joining the squares and matching the corners (remember the centre of Spider's Web?), but the preliminary cutting and stitching is simplified.

This amazing piece of lateral thinking was first devised by American quilter Barbara Johannah and is based on a drawn grid of squares, the size of which depends on the final size required. When planning a machined design which uses 3in (7.6cm) squares finished size, you must cut 3½in (8.9cm) squares to allow for the ¼in (6mm) seam allowance on all sides (Fig 3a). In other words, you always begin with a cut

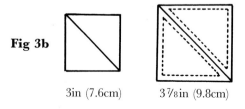

Fig 3a

3in (7.6cm)   3½in (8.9cm)

square which measures the finished size *plus* ½in (1.2cm). For a finished square measuring 3in (7.6cm) made up of two triangles, the starting measurement has to allow for the diagonal seam across the square and must be 3⅞in (9.8cm) square (Fig 3b). In other

Fig 3b

3in (7.6cm)   3⅞in (9.8cm)

words, for your drawn grid you always add ⅞in (2.2cm) to the final measurement. A tiresome business, but one not to be avoided if the work is going to finish up exactly the size you want.

COLOUR CHOICES

Six block designs are shown in Figs 4a to 4f. Each one uses just two fabrics and because the designs are so varied it is quite possible to make more than one block for the sampler quilt without any similarity between them.

CONSTRUCTION

1 From each of the two chosen fabrics cut a piece measuring about 16½ x 9in (42 x 22.8cm). Place them right sides together and press. This will help keep the two layers in place.

LINDY WARD

'I love the colours in old, faded quilts so I selected my materials to give that soft, muted effect now, rather than waiting years for it to happen naturally.'

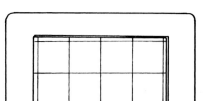

Fig 5

2 Place the two layers of fabric on a cutting board. On the top fabric you are going to draw a grid of eight squares – two rows of four – each square measuring 3⅞in (9.8cm) square (Fig 5). To do this accurately it is better to use the measurements on the ruler rather than those on the cutting board.

Find the line or marks on the ruler that are 3⅞in (9.8cm) from one edge. Mark this distance by sticking a small piece of tape at each end of the ruler on the 3⅞in (9.8cm) line (Fig 6).

3⅞in (9.8cm)

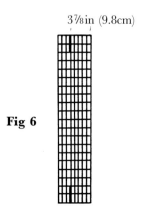

Fig 6

Place the ruler vertically about ¼in (6mm) from the left-hand edge of the fabrics (Fig 7a). Using a marking pencil, draw a line from top to bottom of the fabric along the ruler's edge.

Move the ruler across the fabric to the right until the marked 3⅞in (9.8cm) line is exactly on

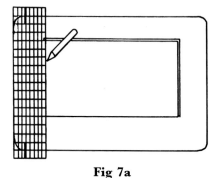

Fig 7a

top of the drawn line (Fig 7b). Draw a line along the ruler's edge.

Once again move the ruler across the fabric to the right until the new drawn line lies exactly under the 3⅞in (9.8cm) line on the ruler. Draw a

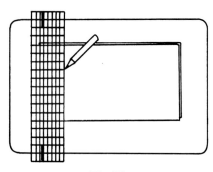

Fig 7b

line along the ruler's edge. Repeat this twice until five vertical lines have been drawn on to the fabric at 3⅞in (9.8cm) intervals. Left-handed quilters should begin marking from the right-hand side and move the ruler across the fabric to the left.

3 Turn the ruler horizontally and draw a line on the fabric about ¼in (6mm) from the bottom edges (Fig 7c). In the same way as before, move the ruler

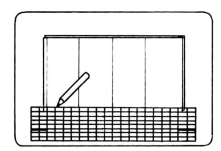

Fig 7c

upwards over the fabric until the 3⅞in (9.8cm) line is exactly on top of the drawn line (Fig 7d). Draw a line along the ruler's edge. Repeat this once more to complete the grid of two rows of four squares.

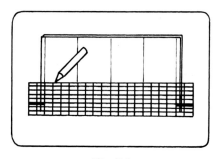

Fig 7d

4 Draw diagonal lines across each square in one direction only (Fig 8).

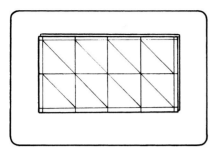

Fig 8

5 Pin the two fabrics together with eight to ten pins to hold the layers while stitching.
6 Machine a line of stitching on *either side* of the drawn diagonal lines at a distance of exactly $^1/_4$in (6mm) using a slightly smaller stitch as usual (Fig 9).

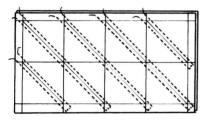

Fig 9

If you have a strip of masking tape stuck on to your machine plate as a stitching guide you will not be able to see it through the layers of fabric, so another way of stitching accurately must be found:

a Use a special $^1/_4$in (6mm) foot on the machine, see Basic Equipment page 10.

b If your machine has the facility, move the machine needle until the distance betwen it and the side of your usual machine foot is exactly $^1/_4$in (6mm).

c Using a different colour marking pencil to prevent confusion, draw in a line $^1/_4$in (6mm) away from the diagonal line on both sides.

7 Once the pairs of lines have been stitched, remove the fabrics from the machine and place them on the cutting board. Using a ruler and cutter, cut along all the drawn vertical lines. Without moving the fabric, cut along the drawn horizontal lines. Finally cut along the drawn diagonal lines (Fig 10). You will find that a miracle has happened and that when you pick up each triangle of fabric, it has been stitched to another and you have a pieced square made of two triangles of two different fabrics. Some of the

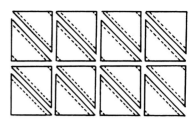

Fig 10

triangles will have a line of stitches across one corner (Fig 11). Loosen these gently by pulling the fabrics apart, they will easily come undone and the threads can be removed.

Fig 11

8 Press each square from the front with the seams towards the darker fabric.
9 Arrange the sixteen squares in your chosen design. If they do not all fit together perfectly, remember that you can swop the squares around because they are all identical.
10 Sew together the top four squares to make a row. If you have a design where two triangles meet in a point, check that once they are joined the two triangles meet in an arrowhead $^1/_4$in (6mm) from the top edges of the fabric (Fig 12), see Spider's Web page 54. From the front press all seams on row one in one direction.

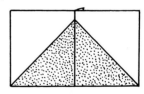

Fig 12

11 Join together the four squares in row two. From the front press the seams in the opposite direction to row one. Join rows one and two, matching seams carefully. Repeat with rows three and four until the block is completed.
12 Press the completed block from the front and measure, it should be exactly $12^1/_2$in (31.7cm) square. If it is not, trim or add a small border, see page 109 for instructions on trimming the blocks and adding borders.
13 Add the framing sashing strips, following the instructions on page 110.

ROSE OF SHARON

Appliqué is a technique often used in quilt-making and many of the traditional appliqué designs, which include simplified flowers, leaves and wreaths, are used together with piecing and quilting to create beautiful quilts.

The appliqué block for the sampler quilt is the Rose of Sharon design, which I chose partly for its good looks and partly because it combines all the possibly tricky elements of appliqué: sharp points, deep V-shapes, curves and overlapping pieces. By

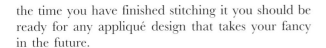

the time you have finished stitching it you should be ready for any appliqué design that takes your fancy in the future.

COLOUR CHOICES

This design gives you a chance to use up all the small pieces of fabric you may have as none of the appliqué pieces are very big, although you will need a 13in (33cm) square of background fabric which will be trimmed down to a 12½in (31.7cm) square once the appliqué has been completed. Cut out and arrange one section of the design on the background square (Fig 2 page 84) before you begin sewing to check that you like the arrangement of fabrics.

CONSTRUCTION

Before beginning any appliqué design you must do some planning. Firstly, the appliqué shapes should always be cut so that when they are sewn in position the straight grain of all the fabrics matches the straight grain of the background fabric. The straight grain is marked on the templates here with a double-headed arrow. Secondly, the appliqué shapes must be attached in the right order so that the top shapes are added last. Where two shapes meet, the seam allowance of the bottom background piece is left unturned. The second piece is then placed overlapping this raw edge. In Fig 2 page 84, the dotted lines indicate where the seam allowances are left unturned and overlapped by another shape. Small arrowheads indicate edges where the seam allowances have been turned under and tacked.

1 Cut a 13in (33cm) square of fabric for the background. Fold it diagonally into four to find the centre point, then finger press. Trace the design layout Fig 2 page 84 on to paper. Place the fabric square over the design layout, positioning the centre of the fabric over the central cross on circle E and a diagonal fold over the broken positioning line. Draw *very* lightly with a marking pencil about ⅛in (3mm) inside the lines of the design to give an indication where the appliqué pieces will be positioned. Do not draw exact outlines in case these show around the edges of the appliquéd shapes after stitching. If the fabric is not fine enough to trace through, use a light box, see Basic Equipment page 10. Turn the fabric and position another diagonal fold over the positioning line on the layout. Draw the guidelines for each shape as before. Repeat this with the other two diagonal fold lines until the complete appliqué design has been marked on the fabric.

2 Make templates A, B D and E from Fig 1 page 84 in the usual way, see page 15 for instructions on making templates. Template C is for the inner flower and is optional. If the fabric for the outer flower D is very busy you may feel that you do not need the extra layer, in which case omit template C.

3 The outlines of the shapes can be transferred to the fabrics in two ways:

a Hold the card template in position on the *front* of the appliqué fabric and draw round it lightly with a sharp marking pencil.

b Draw round the template on the *wrong* side of the appliqué fabric. Place the fabric on a pad of folded fabric, wrong side up. Hold the card template in position on the drawn outline and, using a large blunt-ended needle, run the point very firmly around the edge of the template. This is the needle-marking technique first used in Dresden Plate page 70.

Both these techniques work well so choose whichever one you prefer. You may find that your fabric does not crease well enough for needle-marking, or that a marking pencil does not show clearly on the fabric. Try both methods and use whichever one is the more efficient.

For the design you will need four of shape A, eight of shape B, four of shape C, four of shape D and one of shape E.

4 Once the outlines have been transferred to the appliqué fabric, cut them out adding a ¼in (6mm) seam allowance. Using sharp scissors clip any curved edges at right angles to the pencil line, nearly but not quite to the line itself. Outer points should be left unclipped for ½in (1.2cm) either side of the point while V-shaped edges need to be clipped cleanly to the pencil line (Fig 3).

outer points left unclipped

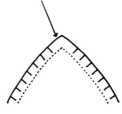

cut right up to line

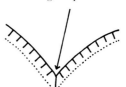

Fig 3

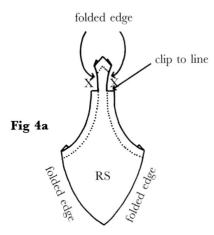

folded edge

clip to line

X X

Fig 4a

folded edge

folded edge

folded edge

RS

5 Begin with shape A; Fig 4a shows the edges that are to be clipped and turned under. Clip to the line at the points marked X so that the narrow stem shape can be turned under. The two unturned edges will be overlapped by shapes B. Turn the appropriate seam allowances to the back after clipping, following the pencil line or needle-marked fold exactly and tack with small running stitches, as in Dresden Plate. Do not press the tacked appliqué pieces as it will be easier to ease out any irregularities in the edges as you stitch if they are unpressed.

6 Clip and tack under all edges of shape B. The sharp corners can be folded over neatly in three stages (Fig 4b).

7 Clip and tack under shapes C (if used) and D on the outer curves only (Fig 4c).

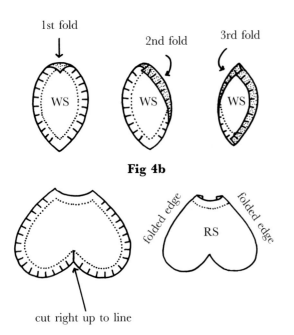

1st fold

2nd fold

3rd fold

WS

WS

WS

Fig 4b

RS

folded edge

folded edge

cut right up to line

Fig 4c

8 Shape E can be made either by gathering the fabric circle around a card template or by using freezer paper. Follow the instructions given in Dresden Plate page 70.

9 Arrange the tacked shapes in position on the background, beginning with A, then B, C, D and finally E. Make sure that each shape overlaps the previous one by 1/4in (6mm). Pin or tack each piece in place (Fig 5).

Fig 5

10 Stitch each shape on to the background with small even slip stitches, beginning with shape A and working towards the centre (Fig 6). Match the sewing threads to the appliqué fabrics, not the background. In the V-shaped areas of any shape, which have been clipped right up to the line, reinforce with two or three stitches in the inner corner (Fig 7).

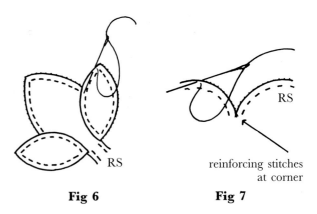

RS

RS

RS

reinforcing stitches at corner

Fig 6   **Fig 7**

11 Once the appliqué has been completed, remove the tacking stitches. If you wish the layers can be reduced by cutting away the background fabric behind the appliqué. This is your choice, although if freezer paper has been used for the central circle then the background fabric has to be cut away so that the paper can be removed.

12 Trim the background fabric to an exact 121/2in (31.7cm) square.

13 Add the framing sashing strips as usual, following the instructions on page 110.

JENNY SPENCER

*'My first quilt, called Golf Widow - now I have my own
obsession! I wanted the effect of an old, faded quilt, so
chose soft, muted colours. When I learned Semonole
Patchwork I couldn't stop, hence the borders.'*

Fig 1 Templates – actual size

Fig 2 Design layout for Rose of Sharon

QUICK MACHINE PATCHWORK

WILD GOOSE CHASE

A BLOCK BASED ON FLYING GEESE

Flying Geese is a favourite pattern, appearing in many quilts both as blocks (Figs 1a, 1b, and 1c) and as borders (Fig 1d). The block for the sampler quilt is called Dutchman's Puzzle, but is also known as Wild Goose Chase, which I prefer as it conjures up the desperate chase for the perfect fabric for the quilt! Traditionally this design was laboriously pieced using templates and American piecing. Pauline Adams, a very clever quilt-maker from Hertfordshire, has worked out this ingenious machined method.

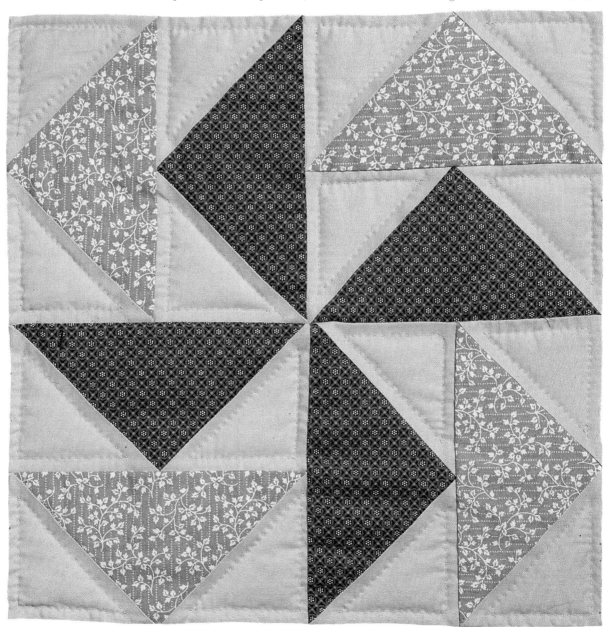

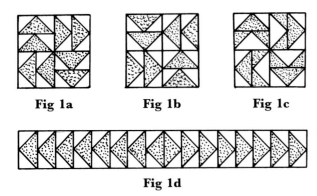

Fig 1a　　　**Fig 1b**　　　**Fig 1c**

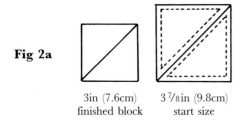

Fig 1d

The quick method of sewing half-square triangles (see page 75) was based on the principle that if you want to finish up with a square of a certain size, you must start with a square that is ⅞in (2.2cm) larger (Fig 2a). This includes the ¼in (6mm) seam allowance round the edges plus the diagonal seam which joins the two triangles.

Fig 2a

3in (7.6cm)　　3⅞in (9.8cm)
finished block　　start size

There is a similar formula for cutting a square divided into four triangles. The final size required needs to have an extra 1¼in (3.2cm) added to it at the start. This extra includes the ¼in (6mm) seam allowance round the edges plus the two diagonal seams (Fig 2b). Do not ask me to explain this: someone has done lots of hard sums to give us this formula, just accept it gratefully. Pauline's method uses both these principles. If you are very mathematical, you may be able to fathom the logic behind it. If you are like me you will just follow the instructions and be amazed at the result.

Fig 2b

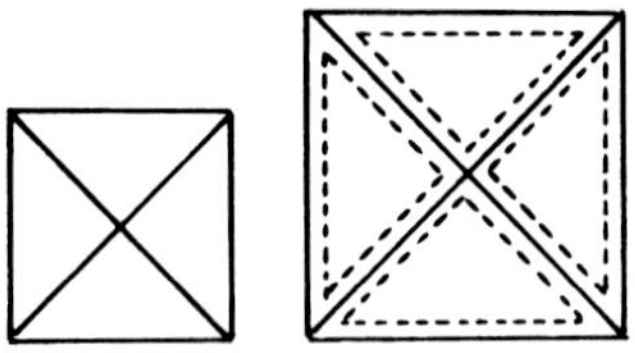

3in (7.6cm)　　4¼in (10.6cm)
finished block　　start size

COLOUR CHOICES

The block uses two main colours for the large triangles, known in the pattern as geese, and one background shade for the smaller triangles, which

represent the sky (Fig 3). When you get to this block you may be running short of some fabrics, so it is best to check with the sizes given below to ensure you have enough for your chosen shades.

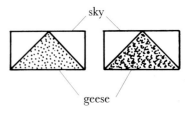

sky

geese

Fig 3

CONSTRUCTION

The design is made from eight Flying Geese, the final size of each unit being 6 x 3in (15.2 x 7.6cm). The large squares are cut 1¼in (3.2cm) larger than the final size: 6in + 1¼in = 7¼in (15.2cm + 3.2cm = 18.4cm) square. The small squares are cut ⅞in (2.2cm) larger than the final size: 3in + ⅞in = 3⅞in (7.6cm + 2.2cm = 9.8cm) square.

1 Cut a 7¼in (18.4cm) square from each of the two fabrics you are using for the 'geese'. Draw the diagonals on the *right side* of each square with a sharp marking pencil (Fig 4).

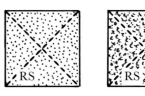

Fig 4

PAM CROGER

'My first sampler quilt. The great thing was the camaraderie within the group. I learned to use fabrics with much more confidence and more boldness.'

2 Cut eight 3⅞in (9.8cm) squares from the 'sky' fabric by cutting a strip 3⅞in (9.8cm) wide and cutting off 3⅞in (9.8cm) lengths (Fig 5). Draw one diagonal on the *wrong side* of each of these (Fig 6).

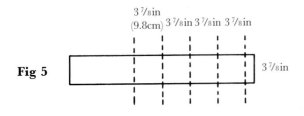

Fig 5

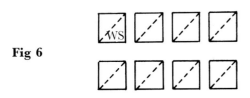

Fig 6

3 With right sides together, pin two of the smaller squares on to one of the larger squares, lining up the drawn diagonal lines. The two corners of the smaller squares will overlap in the centre (Fig 7a). Trim off these corners following the drawn line on the large square so that the two smaller squares meet but do not overlap (Fig 7b).

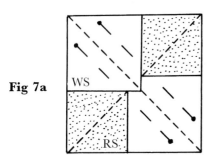

Fig 7a

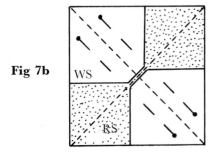

Fig 7b

4 On the smaller squares machine-stitch a seam on either side of the drawn diagonal lines exactly ¼in (6mm) from the line (Fig 8). This is the same technique used in Triangles page 75.

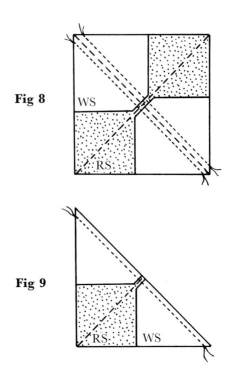

Fig 8

Fig 9

5 Cut along the drawn diagonal line between the two stitched lines (Fig 9).

6 Take one section and finger press the small triangular pieces away from the main triangle (Fig 10).

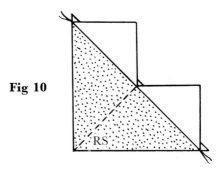

Fig 10

7 With right sides together, pin a small square on to the main triangle, matching the drawn diagonals as before (Fig 11a). Machine a seam on either side of the diagonal line on the small square, exactly ¼in (6mm) from the line (Fig 11b). Cut along the

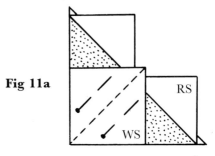

Fig 11a

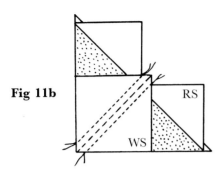

Fig 11b

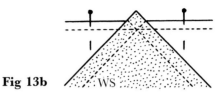

Fig 13b

drawn line between the two stitched lines (Fig 11c).
8 Repeat this with the other section and one small square. Press each piece from the front, with the

the centre (Fig 13b). If you stitch right through this cross of stitches you will not cut off the point of the large triangle. After all, who wants Flying Geese with bent beaks? Press seams to one side from the front of the work (Fig 14).

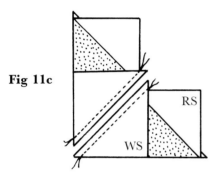

Fig 11c

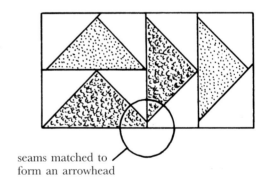

Fig 14

press

seams lying towards the smaller triangles. You will now have four identical Flying Geese (Fig 12a).
9 Repeat the entire process, using the second large square of fabric and the remaining four smaller squares. This will give you four Flying Geese in the second colour combination (Fig 12b).

11 Arrange the four sections in the design. Join the top two together so that the two seams meet in an arrowhead ¼in (6mm) from the edge (Fig 15). Press the seam to one side. Join the bottom pair, pressing the seam in the opposite direction.

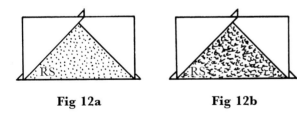

Fig 12a   **Fig 12b**

10 Arrange the eight Flying Geese in the design shown in Fig 1a, or any other arrangement that looks good. Join the Flying Geese into pairs, pinning them as shown in Fig 13a, so that when you stitch you sew through the crossed seams in

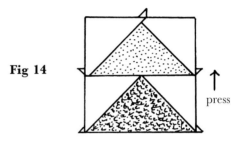

seams matched to form an arrowhead

Fig 15

Sew the two halves together, matching the centre seams carefully. Either press this long seam to one side or press it open, whichever gives a flatter result.
12 Measure the completed block, it should be 12½in (31.7cm) square. If the block is too big, try taking in the seams a little rather than trimming down the outside edges, as losing the sharp points can spoil the design. If the block is too small, add a narrow border to bring it up to size, see page 109 for instructions on trimming and adding borders.
13 Add the framing sashing strips, see page 110 for instructions.

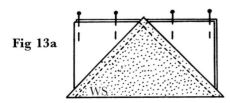

Fig 13a

TULIP BLOCK

Stained glass has been used to enhance the windows of churches and houses for hundreds of years. The depth of colour from light pouring through tinted glass outlined by black leading gives a stunning effect. Stained glass patchwork, which is a variation of hand appliqué, aims to create the same effect with fabric. The coloured sections are tacked in position on the background, then the edges are covered by narrow strips of black fabric to give the impression of stained glass.

COLOUR CHOICES

If you were planning a wallhanging of a stained glass design your chosen fabrics would probably imitate the brilliance and jewel-like quality of true stained glass as closely as possible. However, these strong colours may not be appropriate for the sampler quilt, so just follow the technique using colours that complement the blocks you have already made. The edging round each area of colour can be of any fabric you wish. It does not even have to be a plain colour, striped or patterned fabrics can look wonderful. The background area needs to be a 13in (33cm) square, while the bias strips (strips cut diagonally across the fabric) for the 'leading' can be cut from a piece measuring 14in (35.5cm) square.

CONSTRUCTION

1 Draw a 13in (33cm) square on a large sheet of tracing paper. I do this by laying the paper on a cutting board, using the board markings to find the four corners of the square. I mark these with dots, then join up the dots with a long ruler to make the square. Mark the centre vertical line with a dotted line (Fig 1a) using the same technique. Mark the centre point O on this line.

2 Trace the design in Fig 2 page 92 on to one half of the tracing paper, matching the centre lines and point O. Continue drawing the lines of the design to meet the edges of the paper square (Fig 1b). From point O measure along the centre dotted line 5¼in (13.3cm) above and 5¼in (13.3cm) below. Mark both these points. From each point draw a

horizontal line across the designs to the edge of the paper square. Turn the paper over and trace the other half of the design, matching the centre lines and both halves of the design exactly (Fig 1b). Include the arrows which show the direction of the straight grain of the fabric.

3 Cut a 13in (33cm) square of fabric for the background. Fold it in half vertically and crease it lightly to mark the centre line.

4 Place the fabric square over the design layout, matching the creased line with the central dotted line on the tracing. Trace the design on to the fabric with a sharp marking pencil. Use a light box if necessary, see Basic Equipment page 10.

5 Cut shapes A, B and C (Fig 3) from the tracing paper. Use these as patterns by pinning them on to the right side of the chosen fabrics, matching the grain arrows on the tracings with the straight grain of the fabric (the direction of the woven threads).

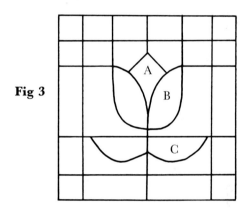

Fig 3

Cut around each shape exactly, no extra seam allowance is needed. Use a single layer of fabric for shape A and a double layer (right sides together) for shapes B and C to give one centre tulip petal, two side petals and two leaves.

6 Pin each piece in position on the background square so that the raw edges of each shape butts against its neighbour. Tack in place (Fig 4).

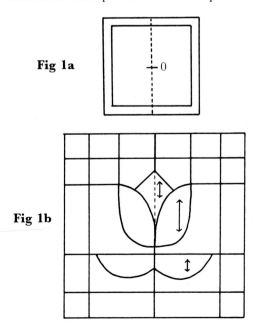

Fig 1a

Fig 1b

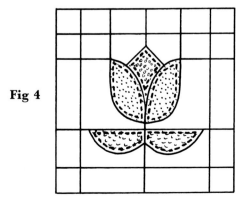

Fig 4

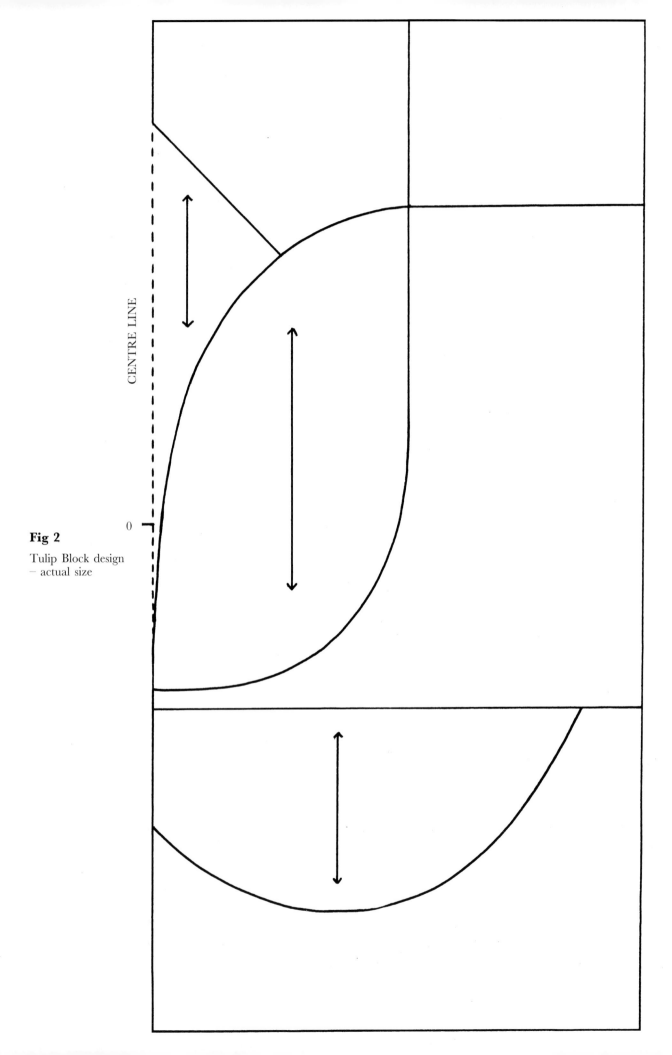

Fig 2

Tulip Block design
– actual size

CENTRE LINE

0

7 The 'leading' strips must be cut on the bias of the fabric because they need to stretch slightly to curve around the shapes without puckering; 1in (2.5cm) wide bias strips are needed for this design.

To cut the strips place a single layer of fabric across one of the 45° lines on a cutting board. Cut along the line with a rotary ruler and cutter (Fig 5). Turn the fabric so that the cut edge is on the left and move the ruler over it until the cut edge lines up with the required width on the ruler. Cut along the right side of the ruler. Repeat this across the fabric (Fig 6). Left-handers should cut their strips from the right, not the left.

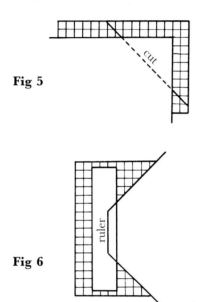

Fig 5

Fig 6

There are two gadgets available which will help quilters make folded bias strips: a Bias-Maker or Bias Bars, see Basic Equipment page 10. Each one uses a different procedure so try them both, if possible, and use whichever you prefer.

With a Bias-Maker, use the ¹⁄₂in (1.2cm) version and follow the manufacturer's instructions for pulling the strip of bias fabric through the gadget. Press the bias strip with a steam iron as it appears in its folded form from the narrower end of the Bias-Maker (Fig 7). This will make a length of bias that looks exactly like commercial bias binding and is about ¹⁄₂in (1.2cm) wide, which is a little too wide for this design. To narrow the folded strip, refold one side across the back and press with a steam iron (Fig 8).

With Bias Bars, use a ¹⁄₄in (6mm) width bar. With wrong sides facing, fold the 1in (2.5cm) wide bias strip of fabric in half. Using a slightly smaller stitch than normal, machine-stitch a ¹⁄₄in (6mm)

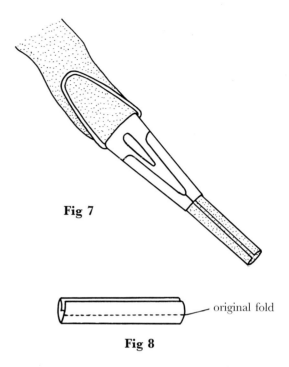

Fig 7

original fold

Fig 8

seam down the length of the strip to make a tube. Always make a short sample length first to check that the Bias Bar will just slip into the tube – it needs to fit really snuggly without any slack (Fig 9a). Trim the seams to a scant ¹⁄₈in (3mm) (Fig 9b). Slide the Bias Bar into the tube, twisting the fabric so that both seam and seam allowance lie across one flat side of the bar and cannot be seen from the other side (Fig 9c). With the bar in place, press the seam allowance to one side. Slide the tube gradually off the bar, pressing firmly as you go.

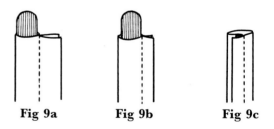

Fig 9a   **Fig 9b**   **Fig 9c**

You do not need a continuous length of bias for the design. The sequence for adding the strips has been planned so that as many bias ends as possible are concealed beneath other strips. The suggested order of stitching the Tulip Block is shown in Fig 10.

8 Take a length of pressed bias tubing slightly longer than line one in Fig 10, using the design (Fig 2) for measurement. Pin the strip so that the drawn line on the fabric lies midway underneath it. Trim the ends exactly to match the end of the drawn line (Fig 11).

9 Matching the sewing thread to the strip, not the

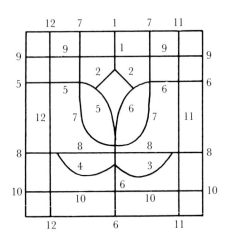

Fig 10

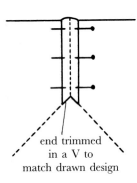

end trimmed
in a V to
match drawn design

Fig 11

background, sew both sides of the strip in turn on to the background with small even slip stitches.

10 Cut a length of pressed bias tubing slightly longer than the V-shaped line two in Fig 10. Fold it into a mitred corner about halfway along and pin in position with the corner covering the end of strip one and the drawn guideline midway beneath it (Fig 12). Trim the ends of the strip to match the ends of the drawn lines. Sew the strip in place on the background.

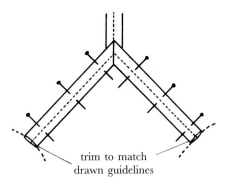

trim to match
drawn guidelines

Fig 12

11 Cut a length of pressed bias tubing slightly longer than line three in Fig 10. This is a curved line, so must be treated slightly differently. The strip must be positioned half on the tacked leaf C and half on the background (Fig 13).

Pin and sew the shorter inside edge of the curve

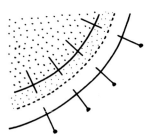

Fig 13

pin and stitch the short edge first

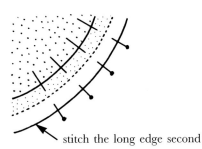

stitch the long edge second

Fig 14

first. The longer outside edge can then be stretched slightly when sewing to fit the curve (Fig 14). If you fix the longer edge first the shorter edge will finish up with little pleats in it. Trim the ends of the strip to match the drawn guidelines.

12 Continue to pin and stitch each length of pressed bias tubing in turn, following the sequence shown in Fig 10.

13 Remove tacking and press. Trim the background fabric to an exact 12½in (31.7cm) square.

14 Add the framing sashing strips as usual, following the instructions on page 110.

COLLIE PARKER

'My enthusiasm for quilting was engendered by the American tradition, especially those quilts which displayed bold colour contrasts and clear designs. In planning my first sampler quilt I tried to choose colours which would produce a quilt that would say "America" to me.'

HAWAIIAN APPLIQUÉ

CROCUS DESIGN

American missionaries introduced patchwork techniques to Hawaii in the 1820s. Since then the native Hawaiians have developed their own colourful interpretation of hand appliqué quilts. Quilt-sized pieces of paper are folded into eighths and then cut to create patterns which represent the flowers, fruit and leaves of the Hawaiian islands. This paper is then unfolded and the pattern used to cut out the huge fabric appliqué motif, which is tacked in place on the contrasting quilt background.

Colours are clear and vibrant like red, green or blue on white and only plain fabrics are used. The appliquéd edges are stroked under with the point of a needle and stitched on to the background in one process. Quilting lines follow the outline of the appliquéd design and are repeated to the edge of the quilt, just like contour lines on a map (Fig 1).

Fig 1

This appliqué technique (known as needle-turning) using a design based on folded paper shapes, can be scaled down and adapted for a block in the sampler quilt. Rather than copy the exotic tropical plants of Hawaii, I felt it was more appropriate to use a design taken from the English garden, in this case a crocus with its characteristic long, pointed leaves. Many students have insisted that the flower is more like a tulip than a crocus, but as there is already a tulip in the stained glass block I am sticking to the crocus label.

COLOUR CHOICES

A 13in (33cm) square piece of background fabric is needed for the background. The appliqué design is cut from a folded 11in (28cm) square of fabric. Just because traditional Hawaiian quilts use strong, plain colours do not feel that you must do the same. An American visiting one of my classes was horrified when she saw the soft colours and patterned fabrics being used with casual abandon as backgrounds or appliqué. As always, use the technique but choose fabrics which suit the balance of your collection of blocks.

CONSTRUCTION

1 With right sides together fold the smaller fabric square (the appliqué fabric) in half (Fig 2a). Fold it

in half again (Fig 2b). Finally fold it diagonally (Fig 2c). Follow Figs 2a, 2b and 2c carefully, and check that the centre of the fabric square is positioned as shown. If it is not you may end up with several pieces of fabric instead of one whole one. Press the folded fabric firmly to give sharp folds.

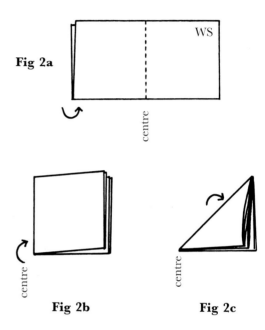

Fig 2a

Fig 2b   **Fig 2c**

2 Make a template of the appliqué design in Fig 3 page 98 by tracing it on to card, or use template plastic, see page 15 for instructions on making templates.

3 Place the template on the folded triangle of fabric, matching the centres. Check that the bias and straight edges of the fabric match the bias and straight markings on the template (Fig 4). Draw round the template using a sharp marking pencil.

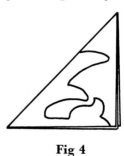

Fig 4

4 Secure the layers of folded fabric with two or three pins. Using very sharp scissors, cut out the drawn outline through all eight layers, holding the fabric firmly so that none of the layers can slip.

5 Fold the background square into eighths in the same way as before. Press lightly with an iron to make guidelines for positioning the appliqué.

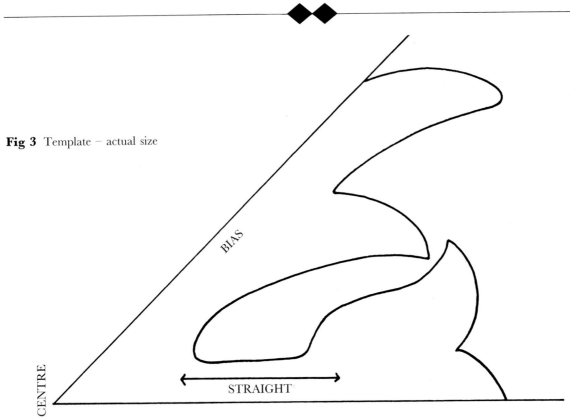

Fig 3 Template – actual size

BIAS

CENTRE

STRAIGHT

6 Unfold the background fabric and lay it on a flat surface. Place the folded appliqué on to the background with the centres matching (Fig 5a). Unfold the appliqué design section by section (Figs 5b and 5c) until the whole design is revealed (Fig 5d). Check that the fold lines on the appliqué design are lying exactly on the guideline folds in the background fabric.

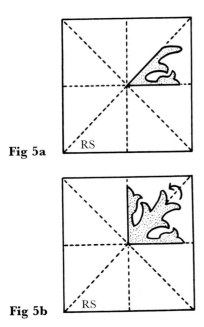

Fig 5a RS

Fig 5b RS

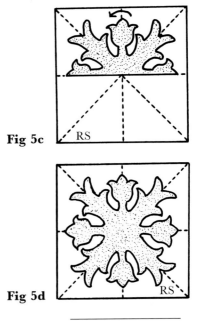

Fig 5c RS

Fig 5d RS

YVETTE LONG

'The colours of the blocks are based on Spring, Summer, Autumn and Winter. This was my first piece of patchwork and I think Lynne nearly died when I told her what I wanted to do! The quilt was used on the cover of the catalogue of the Great British Quilt Festival in 1993.'

7 Pin the appliqué to the background in several places, then tack in place, using ¼in (6mm) long stitches and keeping them about ¼in (6mm) from the edge of the design so that the appliqué is held firmly in place (Fig 6). Press.

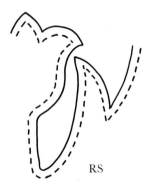

Fig 6

8 Using thread to match the top fabric, turn under and sew the raw edge just ahead of the needle. The turning should be about ⅛in (3mm) and is made by stroking the fabric under with the point of the needle (Fig 7). Sew using small, closely spaced slip stitches.

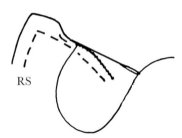

Fig 7

9 When sewing an outside point of the design, work to within ⅛in (3mm) of the point and make a firm stitch (Fig 8a). Using the point of the needle, stroke down the raw edges of fabric away from the last stitch and tuck under the usual ⅛in (3mm) (Fig 8b). Sew the turned edge and continue.

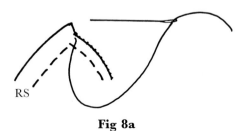

Fig 8a

Fig 8b

10 Do not clip any inner points. Use the needle point to sweep the seam allowance under in a scooping movement. Repeat the movement from side to side until the point becomes rounded and all the seam allowance has been stroked under. Sew the curve with very closely spaced slip stitches (Fig 9).

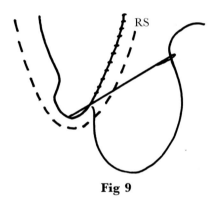

Fig 9

11 Continue turning under and sewing the edge of the appliqué design until it is completely sewn down. Remove the tacking stitches and press.
12 Turn the block to the reverse side and carefully cut away the background fabric behind the appliqué, leaving a seam allowance of ¼in (6mm) beyond the stitch line (Fig 10), see page 26 for instructions. This reduces the layers and makes quilting easier.

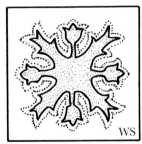

Fig 10

13 Trim the background fabric to an exact 12½in (31.7cm) square.
14 Add the framing sashing strips as usual, following the instructions on page 110.

HONEY BEE

This block and the following design Grape Basket have been included to make up the number of blocks needed to complete the quilt. Neither have brand new techniques to be mastered, so I have deliberately kept the instructions fairly basic so you get used to working on your own.

This particular pieced patchwork design can be worked by hand or machine and incorporates some hand appliqué, so uses the skills you should have acquired so far.

COLOUR CHOICES

Three or more fabrics are used in Honey Bee, so it is a good design for using up scraps. The curved appliqué shapes are meant to represent bees. Presumably the centre Nine-Patch could be a flower or possibly the hive – what does it matter? Just choose the fabrics to suit your quilt, as always, by getting out the blocks you have already completed to see what is needed for balance. This gets easier and easier as there are more completed blocks to relate to. At this stage also, you probably have very little fabric left to choose from, which simplifies the selection process quite a lot!

CONSTRUCTION

This block is usually made by American piecing, using templates and drawing round them. The piecing can then be done by hand or machine. If you wish to use this method, make the templates shown in Fig 1 and proceed as usual for drawing round, cutting etc.

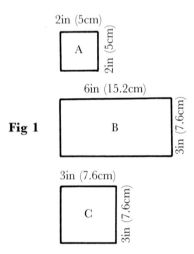

Fig 1

Alternatively, as all the shapes are squares or rectangles, apart from the appliquéd bees, it makes sense to calculate the sizes of the shapes to *include* the seam allowances, cut with rotary equipment and stitch together with machined $^1/_4$in (6mm) seams. This is template-free machined patchwork, like the early block Trip Around The World. To do this you need to look at the *final* measurements of each shape shown in Fig 1. To each measurement add on $^1/_2$in (1.2cm) to allow for the $^1/_4$in (6mm) seam allowance on both sides of the shape. Shape A is 2$^1/_2$in (6.3cm) square, shape B is 6$^1/_2$ x 3$^1/_2$in (16.5 x 8.9cm) and shape C is 3$^1/_2$in (8.9cm) square (Fig 2).

1 Following whichever method of construction you prefer, cut out nine of shape A, five in one fabric,

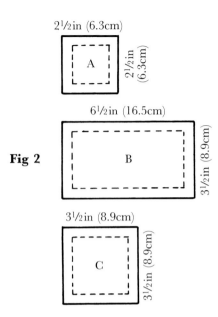

Fig 2

four in another. Cut four of shape B and four of shape C.

2 Assemble the central Nine-Patch square by stitching three rows of three squares each. From the front, press the seams towards the darker fabric (Fig 3a). Join the rows together to make the Nine-Patch square (Fig 3b).

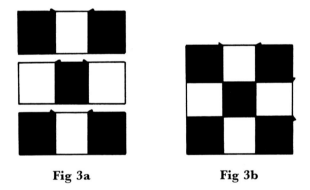

Fig 3a   **Fig 3b**

ANN JONES

'I really loved making the quilt for my son and his wife. The colours were chosen to pick up the colours in their curtain material, some of which I incorporated into the design.'

3 Join on the two side rectangles or B shapes (Fig 4).
4 Stitch together the top row of shapes C, B and C. From the front press the seams towards shapes C (Fig 5). Repeat this to make the bottom row.
5 Join the three rows together, locking the seams so that they match exactly (Figs 6a and 6b).

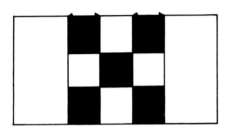

Fig 4

Fig 5

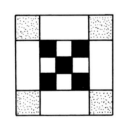

Fig 6a   **Fig 6b**

6 Shapes D and E in Fig 7 represent the body and wing respectively of the bee. The appliqué can be done using freezer paper or by needle-marking the outlines as in Rose of Sharon page 80. Four bee

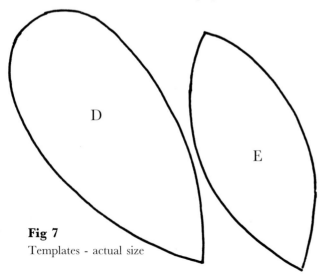

Fig 7
Templates - actual size

body shapes and eight bee wing shapes are needed. If you are needle-marking, make templates of shapes D and E. Needle-mark on the backs of the chosen fabrics and cut out with a ¼in (6mm) seam allowance. Tack under the seam allowances, following the needle-marked creases.

If using freezer paper, trace four bee body shapes and eight bee wing shapes on to the smooth side of freezer paper. Cut out the shapes and iron them, shiny side down, on to the wrong side of the fabrics. Cut out with a ¼in (6mm) seam allowance. Follow the instructions for using freezer paper given in Dresden Plate page 70. If the folded fabric at the pointed sections of the shapes does not tuck flat and shows from the front of the appliqué, either tuck it under while stitching the appliqué on to the background or secure it with a dab of glue from a glue stick. Provided the glue is water-soluble it will not harm your fabric.

7 Arrange the four bee body shapes and eight wings on the pieced block (Fig 8) and pin or tack in place. Sew each one on to the background with small slip stitches, using thread to match the appliqué not the background.

Fig 8

8 Once the appliqué has been completed, the backing fabric can be cut away to reduce the bulk. If it has been traditionally stitched this is a matter of choice, but if freezer paper has been used the back layer has to be cut away so that the paper can be removed.
9 Press the completed block from the front and measure it, it should be 12½in (31.7cm) square. If it does not, trim or add a border, see page 109 for instructions on trimming the blocks and adding borders.
10 Add the framing sashing strips, following the instructions on page 110.

AMERICAN PIECED PATCHWORK

GRAPE BASKET

This is the second of the optional bonus blocks for the sampler quilt. Again there is nothing new in the techniques used to make it, so instructions are fairly basic. Many basket blocks can be found in traditional American patchwork. Some are set as straight baskets, often with appliquéd flowers, others, like the Grape Basket, are set on the diagonal, which adds interest to the sampler quilt. This is a small block, 10in (25.4cm) square, so once completed it needs a frame to make it up to the required 12½in

(31.7cm) square. The pieces are quite small but not difficult to piece and the resulting block will give richness to the quilt. The simplest way to construct Grape Basket is with templates and American piecing by hand or machine.

COLOUR CHOICES

The basket is set on a background fabric and uses two or more fabrics as preferred. Use Fig 1 as a guide for planning your design; make a tracing and shade it in with coloured pencils if this helps. Remember that an extra frame 1in (2.5cm) wide must be added to the design before final sashing.

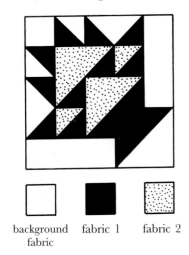

background fabric   fabric 1   fabric 2

Fig 1

CONSTRUCTION

1 Make templates of the five shapes in Fig 2 page 108.
2 On the wrong side of the appropriate fabrics draw round the templates with a sharp marking pencil. Following Fig 1, mark on the background fabric: two of shape A, one of shape B, two of shape C, two of shape D and one of shape E.
  On fabric one mark: twelve of shape C and one of shape E.
  On fabric two mark: two of shape C and two of shape E.
3 Cut out each shape, adding a ¼in (6mm) seam allowance on all sides.
4 This design is not an obvious Four-Patch or Nine-Patch, so the hardest part is sorting out a sequence for piecing. The main design, separated from the two side and final corner sections, is shown in Fig 3. This main block can then be divided into two halves (Fig 4) and each half in sections, as shown in Figs 5a and 5b.

Fig 3

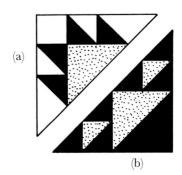

Fig 4

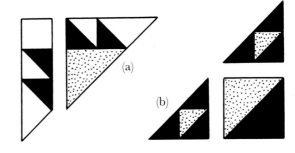

Fig 5a   **Fig 5b**

5 Now join the two halves to make a square (Fig 4). Assemble the two side sections (Fig 3) and join them to the main design square (Fig 6).
6 Finally add the last corner to complete the block (Fig 1).

CHRIS LAUDRUM

'This was my first quilt, called Tickled Pink, and made for my daughter Claire. The border is heavily quilted and edged with folded triangles of fabric, which took far longer than I had planned but was well worth it.'

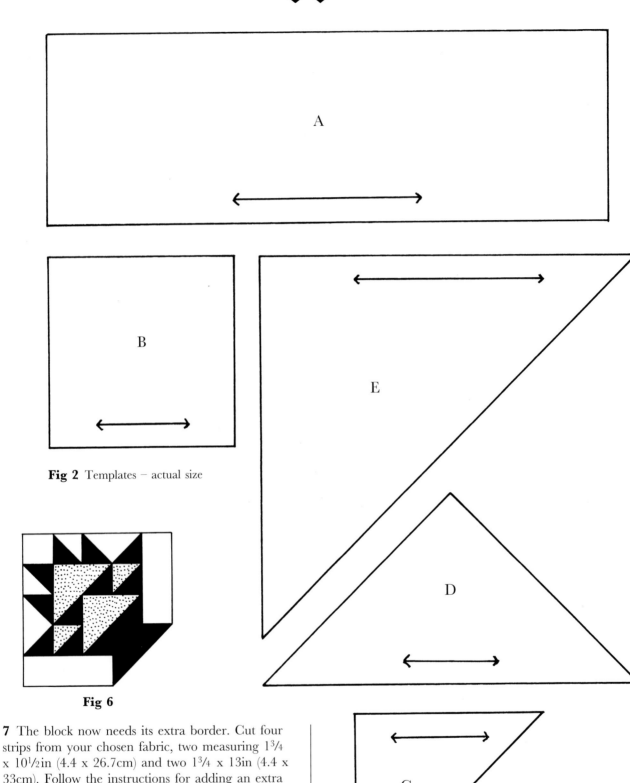

Fig 2 Templates – actual size

Fig 6

7 The block now needs its extra border. Cut four strips from your chosen fabric, two measuring 1³/₄ x 10¹/₂in (4.4 x 26.7cm) and two 1³/₄ x 13in (4.4 x 33cm). Follow the instructions for adding an extra border given in Card Trick page 40.

8 Measure the block, it should be a little larger than 12¹/₂in (31.7cm) square. Trim it to exactly 12¹/₂in (31.7cm) square, see page 109 for instructions on trimming the blocks.

9 Add the framing sashing strips, following the instructions on page 110.

FINISHING THE BLOCKS

Once you have completed all your blocks don't think you can ease off, because there is still plenty more work to be done to finish the blocks before they can be joined together.

TRIMMING THE BLOCKS

Each block should measure *exactly* 12½in (31.7cm) square. If the block is too large it should be trimmed down to the correct size, but do not trim off part of the design and lose corners and points. If necessary try taking in some of the seams within the design to bring it down to size. Blocks like Tumbling Blocks and Dresden Plate can be safely trimmed as only the background squares will be cut into.

To trim down the block, take the completed block and place it on a cutting board with the design centred on a vertical line on the board (Fig 1). From the central line measure 6¼in (15.9cm) to the right, using the markings on the board as your guide. Measure to the left if you are left-handed. Place the ruler vertically on this measurement and trim the fabric (Fig 2).

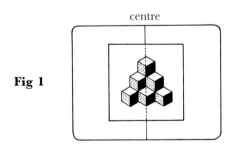

Fig 1

centre

Turn the cutting board through 180° or walk round the table, measure 6¼in (15.9cm) from the centre and trim the opposite side of the fabric square in the same way.

Reposition the fabric on the board so that the trimmed edges are lying horizontally. Centre the design on a vertical line on the board (Fig 3). Trim the left and right edges in the same way as before. Use the marked grid on the cutting board to check that your fabric square is now exactly 12½in (31.7cm).

If the block has finished up smaller than 12½in (31.7cm) square add a narrow extra border to it.

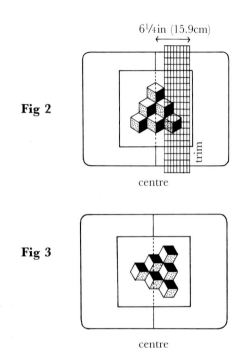

6¼in (15.9cm)

Fig 2

trim

centre

Fig 3

centre

This is not a sign of weakness or ineptitude, in fact several students have done this to their blocks to add to the effect even though their measurements were perfect. To add an extra frame first measure the completed block. If necessary try to reduce the size to 12in (30.5cm) square or less or the extra border will be too tiny to deal with. Some blocks can just be trimmed down as described above, others may need seams within the design taken in to reduce them.

Once trimmed, measure the fabric square. From the fabric chosen for the narrow borders cut two strips to match this measurement by 1in (2.5cm) wide. Pin and stitch these to either side of the block, easing in any fullness if necessary. Press the seams outwards away from the block, ironing from the front of the work (Fig 4).

Measure across the centre of the block from side to side (Fig 5). Cut two strips of the fabric for the narrow border to match this measurement by 1in (2.5cm) wide. Pin and stitch these to the top and bottom edges of the block, easing in any fullness if necessary. Press the seams outwards away from the block, ironing from the front of the work (Fig 6). The block will now measure more than 12½in (31.7cm)

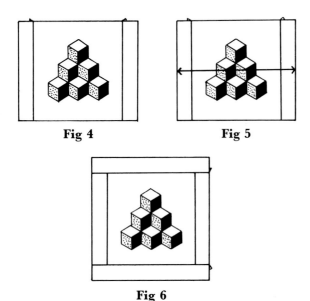

Fig 4   **Fig 5**

Fig 6

square. Follow the instructions for centreing and trimming given earlier. It may seem wasteful to add a strip and then cut some off, but a final trim to size makes a really accurate square.

ADDING THE FRAMING SASHING STRIPS

Once the required 12½in (31.7cm) square is achieved the framing sashing strips can be added. These are cut 1½in (3.8cm) wide. Do not take a long strip and just stitch it on, trimming the end after stitching. The edges of the block may well stretch as you stitch and will no longer measure a true 12½in (31.7cm) square when you finish. Cut the framing strips to size and make the block fit them exactly. From the framing sashing strip fabric cut two strips 12½in (31.7cm) long and 1½in (3.8cm) wide and pin and stitch these to the *sides* of the block. Press the seams outwards away from the block as in Fig 4, ironing from the front of the work.

From the framing sashing strip fabric cut two pieces 14½in (36.8cm) long and 1½in (3.8cm) wide. Pin and stitch these to the *top* and *bottom* edges of the block making the block fit the cut strips exactly and easing in any fullness if necessary. Press the seams outwards away from the block as in Fig 6, ironing from the front of the work.

The final framed block should now measure 14½in (36.8cm) square. If the sashing strips are cut to these measurements each time and the blocks have been trimmed or added to so that they measure exactly 12½in (31.7cm) square, then every block will match the others and there will be no nasty surprises when you start to join them together.

QUILTING

Patchwork quilts are often enhanced by decorative patterns of running stitches known as quilting. These are used to hold the front and back of a quilt together and to keep in place any extra padding that has been sandwiched inbetween. The stitches are made through all the layers to give an attractive design on both sides of the quilt.

Quilting the sampler quilt is done block by block before joining them together, a technique known as 'quilt as you go'. This way the blocks are portable and can be individually quilted once they have been completed, rather than waiting until the whole quilt top is pieced together when you will have to tackle a bed-sized project. You may like to quilt each block once it has been completed before moving on to the next, or you may prefer to wait until several have been made and make a concerted attack on them.

Before tackling any blocks it is a good idea to sew a practice piece first, made up from two pieces of fabric any size you like, with batting between. The Pauper's Block in Fig 1 is an ideal design to quilt for the practice piece as the stitching is continuous from the centre outwards without awkward changes in direction or stops and starts. It also gives you a chance to find out whether you really enjoy hand-quilting and find out how much time you are prepared to devote to it. You need to know this when you start quilting your blocks because each block needs to be quilted about the same amount as all the others to keep the final sizing consistent. If you quilt the first block very densely then you have to do the same to all the others.

WHERE TO QUILT?

Quilting on a piece of patchwork often simply echoes the lines of the patchwork. This may be in the seam-line itself, called 'quilting in the ditch', or more often about ¼in (6mm) away from the seamlines, called 'outline quilting' (Fig 2). Quilting in the ditch can be effective around appliqué shapes or the leading in stained glass patchwork, but otherwise does not add much to the appearance of a block as it sinks into the seam and cannot be seen. Large areas, such as the background to Grandmother's Fan, can be broken up by quilting lines running across them. When I made my sampler quilt, shown on page 2, I limited the quilting to outlining the patchwork segments, sometimes with extra quilting lines parallel to this. Students have since put me to shame by using the most imaginative designs of lines and curves to enhance their blocks. Study the blocks shown in the quilt

Fig 1
Pauper's Block
quilting design

photographs throughout the book to get inspiration.

For curves, put glasses, plates and saucers on the block and draw around the edges, the larger the plate the more gentle the curve. If you feel this approach is beyond you, stick to outline quilting – after all it is the traditional, classic way (never call anything basic or ordinary, the word classic will immediately elevate its status). You can use quilting patterns which are made as plastic stencils, just place them on to the fabric and draw around them. As there is a wide range of chain and cable designs available as plastic stencils in a variety of sizes, they are particularly useful for border designs.

MARKING THE DESIGN

It is best to mark the quilting design on the fabric before the extra layers of batting and backing fabric are added. Outline quilting lines, which are usually

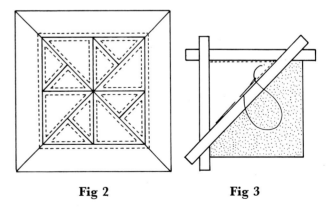

Fig 2   **Fig 3**

¼in (6mm) away from the seamlines, can be sewn by eye or by using masking tape. Stick the tape lightly to the surface of the top fabric with one edge against the seamline. Quilt close to the other edge and remove the tape immediately the stitching has been completed (Fig 3). More complex designs can be drawn out and traced through on to the quilt top, using a light box if necessary, or by drawing straight on to the block. It is important to use a marking pencil that fades or wears off the fabric and does not leave a permanent line, see Basic Equipment page 10.

TACKING THE LAYERS

For each block cut a 15½in (39.4cm) square of the batting and backing fabric, so that both are ½in (1.2cm) larger on all sides than the completed block. Place the backing fabric right side down on a flat surface; you may like to anchor it at the corners with masking tape. Lay the batting on top, patting it into place. Place the block centrally on the batting (Fig 4). Use a long, fine needle and light-coloured tacking thread and tack, using running stitches ¾ to 1in (1.9 to 2.5cm) long, working from the centre of the block outwards across the quilt in a grid of vertical and horizontal lines.

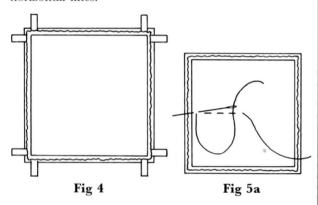

Fig 4   **Fig 5a**

Rather than beginning each tacking line in the centre with a knot, cut enough thread to use right across the block. Begin in the centre, leaving about half the thread as a long end at the start. Tack to the edge, finish with a double stitch and remove the needle (Fig 5a). Re-thread the other end and tack in the opposite direction (Fig 5b). The tacking should be just tight enough to hold the layers together without denting the surface. Continue to tack the horizontal and vertical lines about 3 to 4in (7.6 to 10.1cm) apart to form a grid (Fig 6).

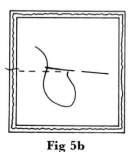
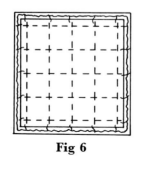

Fig 5b   **Fig 6**

USING A FRAME

In the past small projects were quilted using a quilting hoop. I would recommend one of the newer, square, plastic frames, as they make a convenient shape to fit around the blocks. A tacked block should never be stretched tightly in the frame, adjust the side clips by turning them slightly in towards the block so that the fabric has some 'give' to it, which will make quilting easier. Using a frame really does make the work much smoother and flatter and is virtually essential for quilting large pieces. If you can use a frame for quilting the sampler blocks it will prepare you for any large projects you might make in the future. However, if you are more comfortable working without a frame with the block in your lap, it is perfectly possible to quilt such a small area very successfully in this way provided the block is thoroughly tacked.

STARTING TO QUILT

If you have ever looked closely at the prize-winning quilts at quilt shows you may think that all quilting stitches have to be tiny, even and exquisite. Some are, of course, but many quilts have far larger stitches and are still very effective. What matters is sewing stitches of the same size, which will come as you establish a rhythm. Begin with the Pauper's Block on page 111. As you sew you will find the stitches become more even and you can control the size more easily. Check the back to ensure that the stitches are being made on that side as well, but don't expect them to be exactly the same size. They are usually smaller and as long as you are catching in enough of the back fabric to hold it securely in place that will be fine. With your practice piece do not waste time unpicking poor stitches or you will never establish a good rhythm. Just keep going until you feel you are ready to tackle one of the blocks.

Cut a length of quilting thread about 18in (45.7cm) long. This can provide a contrast to your fabric if you would like it to, or choose a colour which blends with the colours of the block so that any errors are less obvious. Begin quilting in the centre of the block and work outwards. All starting and finishing work is done from the top of the quilt, so make a knot at one end of the thread and push the needle into the top fabric and batting (not the backing) 1in (2.5cm) away from the starting point, preferably further along the line on which you are going to quilt. Bring the needle back up to the surface in position to make the first stitch, which I make a backstitch. Pull gently to pop the knot through the top fabric into the batting.

Starting position: the knot is ready to be popped through into the batting, out of sight.

THE QUILTING STITCH

Each time begin with a backstitch and then a space so that it appears to be a running stitch. When you first quilt it may be easier to make one stitch at a time, but with practice you may increase this to sew two, three or possibly more stitches at a time. If you are quilting without a frame, it is possible to hold the fabric between the thumb and finger of one hand while quilting with the other to manoeuvre the layers. To make the running quilting stitch a reasonable size on both the back and front, the needle must be pushed into the work as vertically as possible and then swung upwards. This is why it is best to use Betweens needles, as they are short and strong and will not bend too easily.

I like to use the top of a thimble to swing the needle up and down. Watch the tension of your stitches by pulling the thread to tighten the stitches just enough to draw the top fabric down but not so much that it puckers. When quilting without a frame, always work from the centre outwards. It may be easier to use several threads at the same time while doing this. If you turn and quilt back towards the middle you may finish up with a bulge or a twist in the fabric in the centre.

If quilting with a frame you need a different approach, because the fabric cannot be gathered and held between your thumb and finger while quilting. Place your free hand under the quilt with the top of your middle finger in the area where the needle should come through the quilt back. Rest the top of the needle against the flat end of the thimble and push the needle vertically through the layers until the tip is just (and only just) touching the underneath

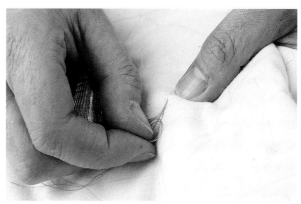

Quilting without a frame: the needle is pushed down vertically into the fabric and swung upwards again to make the stitch.

finger. Press down the layers ahead of the needle with the thumb of your sewing hand.

Push the tip of the needle upwards with the underneath finger. At the same time use the thimble to swing the needle head over and forward to help bring the needle tip to the surface. All this is easier to do than to describe!

The underneath finger supports the vertical needle. The thumb of the top hand presses the quilt layers down.

The top of the needle is swung down to bring the point to the surface.

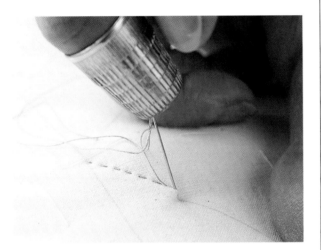

The top of the needle is swung upwards to make the next stitch.

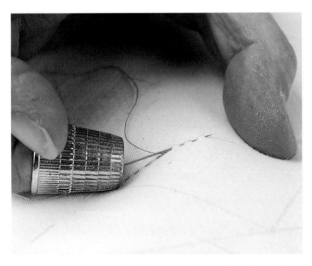

Several stitches can be fed on to the needle before it is pulled through.

Swing the head of the needle upwards to make the next stitch until it is almost vertical and push down with the thimble until the needle tip touches the underneath finger.

Again, use a combination of the underneath finger and the thumb in front of the needle to help force the needle up to the surface of the work while you swing the needle head down on to the quilt top with the thimble. This rocking action can be repeated to make as many stitches on the needle as are comfortable.

Pull the needle through the layers, giving a slight tug on the thread to pull the stitches snugly on to the quilt top. Continue to work in this way until the quilting has been completed.

FINISHING OFF

Finish by either making a knot in the thread close to the surface of the fabric or by winding the thread twice around the needle, inserting the needle into the batting, then running the needle at least 1in (2.5cm) away from the stitching. Pull gently to pop the knot beneath the surface of the top fabric. Cut off the thread level with the quilt top.

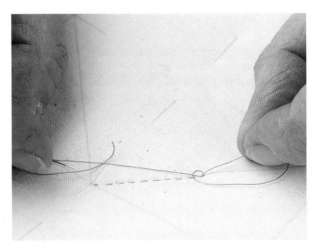

Finish with a knot or by winding the thread twice around the needle and running the needle into the batting for at least 1in (2.5cm).

I use the same technique if I want to move from one part of the design to emerge at another. Finish with a knot, run the thread through the batting and emerge at the new stitching line. Remember to always begin with a backstitch before continuing to quilt.

JOINING THE BLOCKS

Joining the blocks together is not a difficult task but it can be tedious. Still, at least by this stage all the quilting is completed and the quilt starts taking shape like magic as each row is added. The method I use ensures that the joining seams on the back of the quilt reflect those on the front so that the back looks as neat and balanced as possible.

CONSTRUCTION

1 Arrange the completed blocks in your chosen design. Take your time over this and if possible get a second or third opinion, preferably from a fellow quilter. There may, of course, be a block that just does not fit in and you may have to be brave, discard it and make another. Sometimes, though, the block you have felt uneasy about since it was made fits in the final arrangement perfectly. Only at this stage, when all the blocks are laid out and the overall balance established, can you make these decisions.

2 Take the blocks that will make up the top row of the quilt (Fig 1) and place the first two blocks to be joined right sides down. Pull the backing fabric and batting back from the vertical sides to be joined on each block front and pin them out of the way (Fig 2).

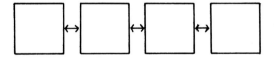

Fig 1

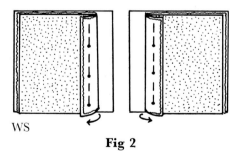

WS

Fig 2

3 With right sides facing, match and pin the two edges of the block fronts together. Machine-stitch them together with a ¼in (6mm) seam allowance (Fig 3). Finger press the seam open and press it lightly with the point of an iron from the *front* of the work. If you try to press it on the back there is a danger of the iron touching the batting and melting it.

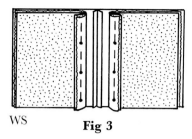

WS   **Fig 3**

4 Lay the joined blocks right sides down on a flat surface. Unpin the batting, but leave the backing fabric pinned back out of the way. Let the two edges of batting overlap each other and cut through both layers along the centre so that the final cut edges butt together. It does not matter exactly where this cut is made as it will be hidden by the fabric. If you are nervous about accidentally cutting the front of the blocks, slide an ordinary 12in (30.5cm) ruler between the batting and the block front before you cut so that your scissors cannot come into contact with the block beneath (Fig 4).

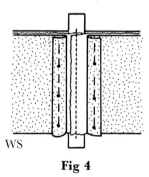

WS

Fig 4

5 Keep the ruler between the layers while you stitch the two butted edges of batting together. I use a large herringbone stitch as it helps to keep the edges flat (Fig 5).

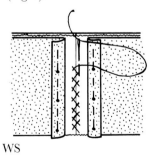

WS

Fig 5

6 Remove the ruler and turn over the joined blocks so that they are now right sides upwards. Push a line of pins through the joining seam and batting from the front. They should be pushed right through so that their points stand upright

115

when the quilt blocks are turned over. Avoid using glass-headed pins for this task, as the heads roll sideways and prevent the pins from remaining upright (Fig 6a).

7 Turn the blocks over with the backing fabric facing upwards (Fig 6b). Fold each piece of backing fabric so that the folded edge butts up to the line of pins. Finger press the fold and trim any excess fabric to the 1/4in (6mm) seam allowance (Fig 6c).

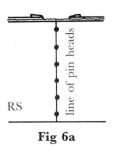
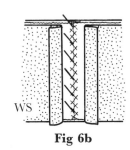

Fig 6a   **Fig 6b**

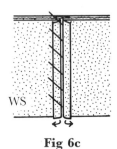

Fig 6c

8 Remove the pins. Unfold the backing fabric of block one and smooth it flat on the batting (Fig 7a). Unfold the backing fabric of block two and *refold* it so that the seam allowance is turned *under*. Match the fold of block two to the creased line of block one (Fig 7b). Pin together, again putting a

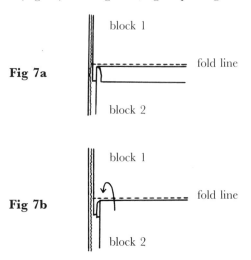

Fig 7a

block 1
fold line
block 2

Fig 7b

block 1
fold line
block 2

ruler under the seam, this time to avoid sewing into the batting.

9 Sew along the overlapping seam with a slip stitch or blind hemming stitch. You can remove the ruler to sew most of this seam, but keep it in place for the first and final 2in (5cm). It does not matter if the stitches penetrate the batting along this seam in the middle areas, but the end 2in (5cm) have to be kept in separate layers so that they can be joined to the next row of blocks (Fig 8).

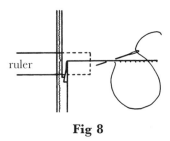

ruler

Fig 8

10 Repeat this process to join all the blocks in the top row. Check that the backing fabric is not pulled too tight and that the front sashing strips are well matched and lying flat. At this stage there is time to adjust the back seams if they are pulling too tightly.

11 Join the blocks in each horizontal row in the same way (Fig 9).

12 Now join the horizontal rows in exactly the same way, matching seams and borders carefully (Fig 10). The quilt is now ready for its borders and final binding.

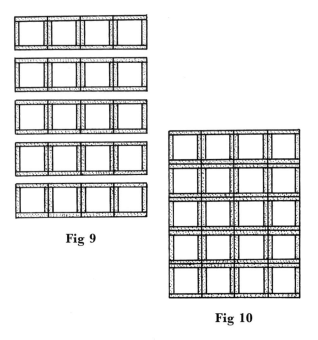

Fig 9

Fig 10

MAKING UP

When work on the individual blocks has been completed, and the quilt top has been joined together, you need to start thinking about the borders before moving on to the final step, binding the quilt edges.

BORDERS

When the quilt top has been joined together you need to start thinking about the border. Put it in position on an appropriate-size bed to see how wide the borders need to be. If the quilt is just going to cover the top of the bed, like an eiderdown, it may not need any extra borders.

When I started making my own sampler quilt I wanted it for a single bed. With twenty blocks the width was fine but I needed more length, so rather than make more blocks, I added a pieced border at the top and bottom of the quilt before adding the final 4in (10.1cm) wide strip of patterned fabric on all sides (see page 2). If I had added the pieced border to the sides as well as to the top and bottom it would have fitted a double bed.

Study all the photographs in this book – they are all the genuine article: quilts made on my sampler course, often by complete beginners. Some of them have complex and imaginative borders, others just a simple double border of complementary fabrics which set off the quilt beautifully. As always, the choice of what kind of border you make is entirely yours and yours alone.

You may be severely restricted in your choice of fabrics by this time. Pieced borders using all the left-over scraps may be the answer, or you could use totally new fabrics. It does not matter if a fabric has not been used in the quilt, as long as it looks as though it belongs.

Plain borders cry out to be quilted, although wide patterned borders – if they form the drop down each side of the bed – can look good without quilting. If you have really had enough by this time then add simple borders and keep quilting to a minimum.

At this stage it is easiest to make the borders and join them to the front of the quilt only and not to the batting and backing. Ignore the back until all the extra pieces – apart from the final binding – have been added to the quilt top.

STRIP BORDERS

A simple framing border of one or more strips of fabric is very effective (Fig 1). If there is not enough fabric to cut strips for the length of the quilt, you can get away with a few joins, provided they look planned. The inner border can have a joining seam in the centre, even if the fabric is a plain one so the

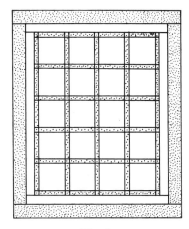

Fig 1

seam looks obvious, as the centre placing of the seamline looks balanced (Fig 2a). Try to avoid making a joining seam in the same position in the next border as it will look clumsy. If possible use a patterned fabric and make two joins at equal distances from the centre so that if they are noticed at all, the joins will look planned and balanced (Fig 2b). If you do not have any suitable fabric left for the outer border you may have to go out and buy something special. At this stage it may seem an extravagance, but any fabric left over will always come in useful

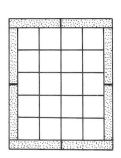

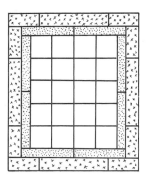

Fig 2a   **Fig 2b**

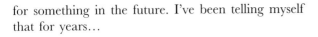

for something in the future. I've been telling myself that for years...

CONSTRUCTION

1 Lay the quilt top on a flat surface and carefully measure the length of the quilt down its *centre*, not along the edge (Fig 3). If you always do this and cut the borders to match the centre measurements there is no danger of the quilt edges spreading with the resulting curse of the quilt-maker: wavy borders.

2 Measuring the length of the quilt exactly, cut two strips of the chosen width to match this measurement for the sides. Pin back the batting and backing fabric out of the way and pin and machine-stitch each side strip to the quilt top, easing in any fullness in the quilt. This is easiest to do if you put the quilt on to a flat surface and match the centres and both ends first before pinning the rest. Press the seams outwards, away from the quilt top (Fig 4).

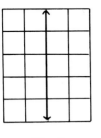

Fig 3   **Fig 4**

3 Measure the width of the quilt from side to side across the centre (Fig 5). Cut two strips of border fabric of the required width to match this measurement. Pin and machine-stitch these to the top and bottom of the quilt, matching the centres and both ends and avoiding the batting and backing as before. Press the seams outwards away from the quilt top (Fig 6).

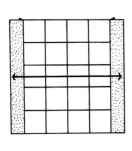

Fig 5   **Fig 6**

4 If another border is planned, measure the quilt across its centre and cut strips to match. Attach the border strips in exactly the same way as before, sides first, then the top and bottom strips (Fig 7).

5 You may prefer to make the borders with squares in the corners (Fig 8). These could be made in the same fabric as the rest of the border or in a contrasting fabric. Squares placed like this appear in Honey Bee (page 101) and are known as cornerstones, they are much easier to make than you would think.

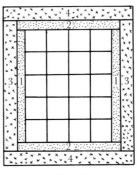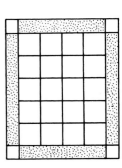

Fig 7   **Fig 8**

First measure the quilt across the centre in *both* directions and cut strips of the required width to match these measurements. Machine-stitch the side strips only on to the quilt as usual. Press the seams outwards away from the quilt top.

Cut four squares of fabric for the corners measuring the same as the cut width of the border strips (Fig 9a). Machine-stitch one of these to either

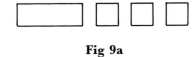

Fig 9a

HAZEL HURST

'Scraps of green fabric were the basis of this quilt with one floral print added to most of the blocks.
The border is made up of machine-pieced units, which were a problem because of an error with my maths.
This was solved by adding an extra unit, then the corners fitted perfectly.'

end of both the top and bottom border strips (Fig 9b). Press seams towards the long strip.

Pin these border strips to the quilt top, matching the seams carefully. Because the seam allowances are lying in opposite directions they will lock together (Fig 9c). If a second border with cornerstones is planned, remeasure the quilt after the first border is added and repeat the process (Fig 10).

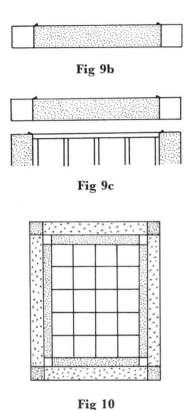

Fig 9b

Fig 9c

Fig 10

PIECED BORDERS

Pieced borders are usually the direct result of finding little left to work with other than a large assortment of scraps, they may mean more work but they can greatly enrich your quilt. This could be the point in your quilt-making career when you learn the meaning of the word 'random'. It is unlikely that there will be enough of all the fabrics to create a pattern and repeat it slavishly. You will probably have to juggle with the cut pieces until you reach a pleasing arrangement. As you will have already done this twenty times when choosing the fabrics for each block, this will not be such a daunting task as it may have been when you started.

At this stage the outer edge of your quilt will have only one width of sashing strip around it. With a busy pieced border you may find that a second

sashing width needs to be added to the quilt before the border is stitched in place. If this is the case, cut and join the sashing strips to the quilt top following the instructions for strip borders given earlier.

Both squares and rectangles can be used to make a pieced border. Figs 11a and 11b show suggested designs for using cut squares; 2½in (6.3cm) cut squares are a comfortable size and should fit mathematically around the quilt. If not, position a seam at the centre of the quilt and trim the two ends to make matching rectangles (Fig 12). Fig 13 shows a design

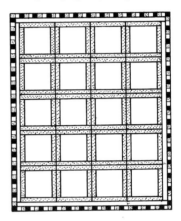

Fig 11a

Fig 11b

Fig 12

using 2½in (6.3cm) wide rectangles – cut any length you like – around the quilt.

The quick machined technique for Flying Geese makes a spectacular border and is well worth the effort (Fig 14a). Measurements need to be adjusted so that the 'geese' fit the quilt blocks, which should have a finished size of 14in (35.5cm) square. The size

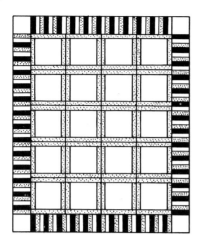

Fig 13

of a Flying Geese border block is 7 x 3½in (17.8 x 8.9cm), four 'geese' should fit each quilt block (Fig 14b). The adapted measurements for these Flying Geese are: large square cut 8¼in (21cm); small squares cut 4⅜in (11.1cm). See page 85 for the instructions on Flying Geese.

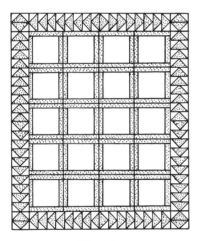

Fig 14a

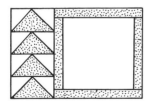

Fig 14b

Once you have decided on the border design, take measurements from the quilt and follow the instructions for joining the pieced strips to the quilt top given earlier. If the design can be used to make the four corners of the border, as in Figs 11a and 11b,

it will make a stunning frame to the quilt. Otherwise incorporate cornerstones (Fig 13).

You may want to add another frame beyond the pieced border. Lay the quilt top on a flat surface and measure it again. Work from these measurements when cutting the new strips. If you keep a tight control on the length of each border strip as you add it, you will finish up with a beautifully flat quilt without a hint of a wave or ripple.

BACKING THE BORDERS

Once all the borders have been completed and joined to the quilt top, turn the whole thing over. An extra strip of batting which extends at least ½in (1.2cm) beyond the quilt, must be added to the original batting on all sides. Join the batting with herringbone stitch along the butted edges in the same way as when joining the blocks (page 115). Strips of the backing fabric can then be machine-stitched to the back of the quilt to make it the same size as the batting. Join the side pieces first and then the top and bottom strips. Take care not to catch any batting in the stitching. Press the seams outwards as usual.

Any quilting in the border areas should be done at this stage, tacking the layers together thoroughly before quilting. Although the quilt is cumbersome now, at least the extra quilting is all around the edge so should not be too difficult to get at. When all the quilting is done (or none, if that was your choice), trim all the layers to match the front of the quilt before the final binding – nearly there!

BINDING

There are many ways to finish the raw edges of a quilt and not every quilt needs the same treatment. However, I do suggest that the sampler quilt is finished with the pressed binding described here as it is easy to apply and always looks good. This binding is made from strips of fabric cut along the straight grain of the fabric, not the bias; bias is only necessary if the edge to be bound is curved.

COLOUR CHOICES

Only about ½in (1.2cm) of binding shows on the final edge of the completed quilt, but it is surprising how important it is to use the right fabric. It can match the border fabric or be another fabric completely. As always, seek some opinions. This is the last colour decision you will have to make about this quilt and it may not be easy. You may also have very little fabric left to choose from. If this is the case, consider cutting 2in (5cm) wide strips of all the scraps you have left, then cut them up into pieces each 2 to 4in (5 to 10.1cm) in length (Fig 1a). Join the pieces together to make a multi-fabric strip which is then used to bind the quilt (Fig 1b). This is economical and can be very effective as long as the borders of the quilt are not already very busy.

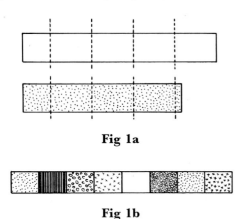

Fig 1a

Fig 1b

CONSTRUCTION

1 Once all the borders have been added and the quilting completed, trim any excess batting and backing fabric level with the edges of the quilt top.
2 Cut four strips of fabric each 2in (5cm) wide for the binding. Two strips, for the sides, should measure the length of the quilt from top to bottom. Two strips, for the top and bottom edges, should measure the width of the quilt from side to side plus 1½in (3.8cm).
3 With wrong sides together, fold each strip in half lengthwise and press (Fig 2a). Open out each pressed strip and bring in the raw edges to the centre crease (Fig 2b). Press the edges. Finally fold in half again and press (Fig 2c).

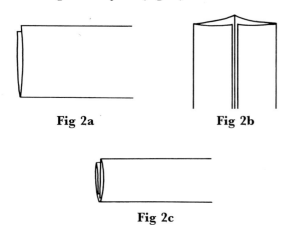

Fig 2a   **Fig 2b**

Fig 2c

4 Take one of the binding strips for the side edges. Open it out and, with right sides together, pin it to one long side of the quilt with the raw edge of the binding extending very slightly above the raw edge of the quilt (Fig 3a). This will help accommodate the thickness of all the layers when the binding is folded over the quilt edge.
5 Machine-stitch along the top crease line through all the layers (Fig 3b). This is easier to do if a

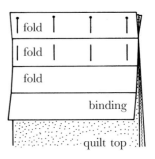

Fig 3a

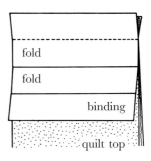

Fig 3b

walking foot is used, see Basic Equipment page 10, as it helps to prevent the layers from creeping and shifting as you stitch.
6 Fold the binding over to the back of the quilt so that the centre crease in the binding matches the raw edges of the quilt. Slip stitch the third folded edge in place along the machine-stitched line on the reverse side of the quilt (Figs 3c and 3d). Trim the ends of the binding to match the quilt exactly.

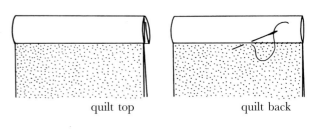

quilt top   quilt back

Fig 3c   **Fig 3d**

7 Bind the opposite side of the quilt in exactly the same way.

8 Pin and machine-stitch the binding to the top and bottom of the quilt in the same way, leaving about ³⁄₄in (1.9cm) of binding extending beyond the quilt at each end (Fig 4a). Trim this extra length back to about ¹⁄₂in (1.2cm) and fold in over the quilt edge (Fig 4b). Turn the binding over to the quilt back and slip stitch in place (Fig 4c). Take care to keep these corners really square before you stitch them.

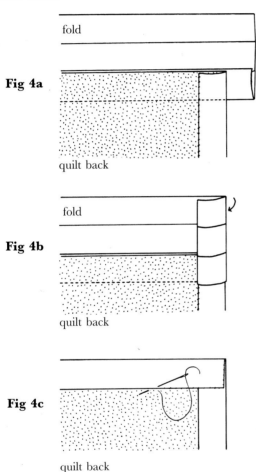

fold

Fig 4a

quilt back

fold

Fig 4b

quilt back

Fig 4c

quilt back

THE FINISHING TOUCH

When the quilt is complete make sure that you put your name and the date on it. This is important for future quilt documentation. Remember that your quilt is a potential heirloom and should be labelled so that its origins are not lost in the mists of time. On the back of the quilt or on a separate piece of fabric write your name and the date with a marking pencil, embroider it in place, using backstitch or chain stitch. Alternatively use one of the special marking pens now available. You can even type your label. The fabric used for writing or typing on can be strengthened by ironing it to a piece of freezer paper. Once the writing has been done, remove the freezer paper and stitch the label in place on the back of the quilt. If your design allows, you might consider quilting or embroidering your name and details on the front of the quilt to make a feature within the overall design.

TAKING CARE OF YOUR QUILT

Do not be too apprehensive about washing your quilt. A well-made quilt will wash and wear wonderfully and if, in time, it shows signs of age that is all part of the charm. Ideally you will have tested any strongly-coloured fabrics for colour-fastness (see page 9) before you began. Check any questionable fabrics by washing left-over scraps in hot water. If the colours run, the safest solution is to take the quilt to a specialist dry cleaner and discuss it with them.

If your washing machine is large enough to hold the quilt comfortably, put it in and use a low temperature programme and a mild washing agent. A short spin will remove some of the excess water which makes the quilt so heavy at this stage.

If you choose to wash the quilt by hand, use the bath and agitate the quilt gently with your hands. Do not let it soak in the water for any length of time. Rinse several times in the bath until the water runs clear. Press out as much rinsing water as you can, whilst the quilt is still in the bath. Press towels against the quilt to absorb as much of the excess water as you can before removing it from the bath.

If possible dry the quilt flat, using a layer of towels or sheets underneath it. A shady flat area outside or an inside floor is ideal, although you may have to patrol outside to fend off the cats and birds! Always keep the quilt out of direct sunlight, as this can fade the colours, even in what is laughingly known as an English summer.

If the quilt needs to be pressed at all, use a cool iron without steam and just press the unquilted sections where creases may show. A hot iron can cause synthetic batting to bond to the fabric, so approach the task with caution, testing for the right heat level for your particular quilt.

Beware of the action of sunlight streaming through a bedroom window on to the quilt. Even in temperate climates, the sun fades fabrics and can spoil a quilt, especially if only a section has been in the sun and it has faded in patches. Always take preventative action from the start.

PROJECTS

Once your sampler quilt has been completed you can start to think about other
ways of using your favourite blocks. These five projects have been developed
from some of the blocks, using both hand and machine techniques, and
graduate in scale from a cushion to a cot quilt, a lap quilt, a quillow and finally
a single bed quilt. I hope they provide you with some ideas of how a particular
block can be expanded into a larger piece, and will inspire you to develop your
own ideas. By all means follow them exactly, or alternatively adapt them. They
are there to give you confidence to create your own designs and interpretations
of the techniques given in this book.

PROJECT 1

GOLDEN QUILTED CUSHION

This design was created with a present for a Golden Wedding Anniversary in mind, hence the colour and the design of interlocking hearts. Raw silk was used for the main cushion with a toning shade for the framing border. Do not be frightened of using silk – it is a joy to quilt and its light-reflecting quality makes even a simple quilting design look wonderful.

FABRIC REQUIREMENTS

20in (50.8cm) silk for the main panel and cushion back
Four strips of border fabric, each measuring 19¹/₂ x 3in (49.5 x 7.6cm)
Piece of 2oz batting 19¹/₂in (49.5cm) square
Fine cotton fabric 19¹/₂in (49.5cm) square to back the quilted cushion top
Cushion pad 20in (50.8cm) square
Final size of cushion: 18¹/₂in (47cm) square

CONSTRUCTION

1 Take a piece of tracing paper 12in (30.5cm) square. Fold it into quarters. Open it out and place it over the design shown in Fig 1 page 126 with point O at the centre and the two dotted lines matching the folds in the tracing paper (Fig 2a). Trace the design on to one quarter of the tracing paper.

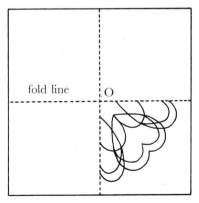

Fig 2a

Move the tracing paper round 90° and fix point O at the centre with the two dotted lines matching the folds of the adjacent quarter of tracing paper (Fig 2b). Trace this section of the design on to the paper. Repeat this for the other two quarters of tracing paper to complete the design.

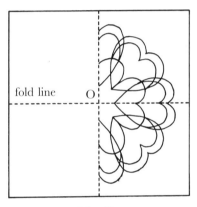

Fig 2b

2 From the main cushion fabric cut a 13¹/₂in (34.2cm) square. Fold it into four and crease lightly to find the centre.
3 Trace the design on to the fabric, using a light box if necessary. The creased lines will help to position the design centrally on the fabric.
4 Now add the border, before the layers are assembled for quilting. The corners on the cushion should be mitred, which is not as daunting as it seems. If you recoil in horror at the prospect, however, a border with cornerstones is perfectly acceptable, see borders page 117 for full instructions.

To make mitred corners, cut four strips of border fabric of the chosen width, each measuring the same length as the main square plus twice the width of the strip (this extra is for the mitred corners). For this project the four strips should each be 3in (7.6cm) wide and 13¹/₂in (34.2cm) plus twice 3in (7.6cm) long, which makes a total length of 19¹/₂in (49.5cm).

On the wrong side of the cushion square mark

Fig 1 Templates – actual size

6 With right sides together, fold the cushion square diagonally, so that the long edges of the two border strips are aligned exactly (Fig 4a).

7 Using a rotary ruler, place the 45° angle line marked on the ruler on the stitching line and the edge of the ruler on the fold of the cushion fabric. Draw a line on the top strip along the ruler's edge from the stitching line to the outer edge (Fig 4b).

Fig 3a

WS

¼in (6mm) in from each corner (Fig 3a).

5 With right sides together, match the centre of one side of the cushion square to the centre of one of the border strips, pin together. Beginning and ending at the marked dots ¼in (6mm) away from the corners of the cushion, machine-stitch together. Backstitch at the start and finish to secure the seams (Fig 3b). Join the remaining three border strips to the cushion in the same way.

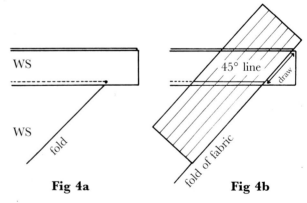

WS

WS

WS

fold

45° line

draw

fold of fabric

Fig 4a   **Fig 4b**

Remove the ruler and pin the two strips together. Machine-stitch along the drawn line. Repeat for each corner. Trim seams to ¼in (6mm), press open. Press the cushion square and borders from the front.

8 Place the cushion square on the batting and backing and tack together ready for quilting. Follow the instructions for tacking the layers together and hand-quilting on page 110. I used silk thread in a slightly darker tone on the gold fabric. Extra quilting lines can be added to frame the design.

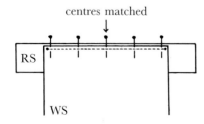

centres matched

RS

WS

Fig 3b   WS

9 For the back, cut two pieces each 19½ x 12in (49.5 x 30.5cm) from the fabric used for the main cushion. Press a ¼in (6mm) turning to the wrong side of the fabric on one long side of each piece. Fold over this edge again to make a ½in (1.2cm) turning (Fig 5a). Machine-stitch along this edge close to the fold (Fig 5b).

10 Place the quilted cushion front on a flat surface right side up. Arrange the two back pieces right

sides down with their raw edges matching the edges of the cushion front and the folded edges overlapping across the centre (Fig 6a).

11 Pin the front and back together and machine-stitch all around the outer edges with a ½in (1.2cm) seam. Trim the seam allowance, cutting the corners to reduce the bulk (Fig 6b).

12 Turn the cushion through to its right side and press the outer seam. Machine-stitch a line ⅜ to ½in (9 to 12mm) from the edge all round the cushion. This gives an extra finish to the cushion.

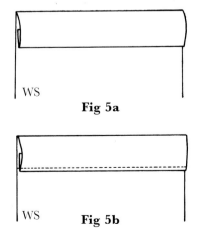

Fig 5a

Fig 5b

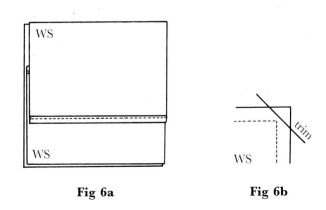

Fig 6a

Fig 6b

PROJECT 2

LOG CABIN COT QUILT

For the sampler quilt four squares of Log Cabin were made at once and then joined to make the block. Here the same basic instructions are followed, this time using the same strip measurements to make twenty-four Log Cabin squares. These are then arranged in the diamond design known as Barn-Raising. A wide toning border completes the quilt which is then quilted.

COLOUR CHOICES

For this particular quilt I used three yellow print fabrics and three blue print fabrics, plus an extra blue fabric which was used for the central squares and the binding. It is also possible to use just two yellow and two blue fabrics and alternate them as described in the Log Cabin instructions, page 63.

FABRIC REQUIREMENTS

Two or three yellow, medium-weight, cotton fabrics totalling 1yd (91.4cm)
Two or three blue, medium-weight, cotton fabrics totalling 1yd (91.4cm)
10in (25.4cm) blue fabric for centres and binding
1yd (91.4cm) extra of one of the yellow prints for borders and backing
Piece of 2oz wadding 29 x 40in (73.5 x 101.5cm)
Final size of quilt:
26½ x 37in (67.3 x 94cm)

CONSTRUCTION

1 Make four Log Cabin squares following the instructions given in Log Cabin, page 63.
2 Make four more squares, but change the order of the fabrics as you use them (Fig 1).
3 Continue to make Log Cabin squares, four at a time, alternating the arrangement of fabrics so that of the final twenty-four squares twelve are in the first arrangement and twelve in the second. By alternating the squares in the final layout you avoid having two strips of the same fabric placed next to each other.

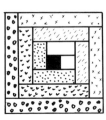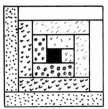

Fig 1

4 Check the size of each finished square by placing it on the grid on a cutting board. They will probably vary in size and at this stage it is possible to cut off narrow strips from the edges of any that are too big. Small squares should have their last two strips re-stitched with narrower seams to help increase the final size. Do not be disheartened – these squares involve so many seams that it would be a miracle if they all matched each other.
5 Arrange the squares in the design shown in Fig 2. Swop individual squares around so that the sizes match as nearly as possible. You will find that all the odd ones finish up around the outside edge and on the corners!

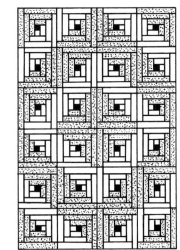

Fig 2

6 Machine-stitch the squares into rows (Fig 3), pressing the joining seams of each row in alternate directions to help lock the seams (Fig 4). Place each row back with the others to check that the layout of the design is still correct. It is so easy to place one square the wrong way and not notice until the

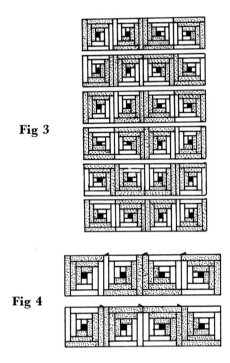

Fig 3

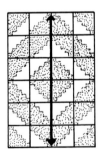

Fig 4

last stitch in the quilt has been made. The final long seams can be pressed to one side or, if this seems too bulky, press the seam allowances open.

7 Measure the length of the quilt down its centre, not along the edge (Fig 5). From the border fabric cut two strips to match this measurement and 3in (7.6cm) wide. Pin and stitch these strips to each side of the quilt, easing any fullness in the quilt to fit the border strips. Press the seams outwards, away from the quilt (Fig 6).

Fig 5

Fig 6

8 Measure the quilt from side to side across its centre (Fig 7). From the border fabric cut two strips to match this measurement and 3in (7.6cm) wide.

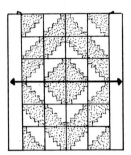

Fig 7

Pin and stitch these strips to the top and bottom of the quilt, easing any fullness in the quilt to fit the border strips. This way the border will retain the measurement of the quilt centre and not spread at the edges. If you see a quilt with wavy edges where there is obviously too much fullness, it is because the border strips have not been cut to size before joining them on to the quilt. Beware!

9 Cut the backing fabric to match the batting by laying the batting on it and cutting around the edges. If the piece for the back of the quilt is not large enough, add strips of whatever you have left (apart from the binding fabric). This will give the quilt a patchwork back which makes it even more interesting.

10 Tack the three layers together ready for quilting. Quilting through all these seams will not be easy, so aim for even stitches and do not worry about size too much. The quilting design is shown in Fig 8, for general instructions on quilting see page 110.

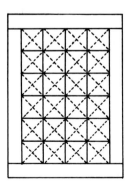

Fig 8

11 Once the quilting has been completed, trim the wadding and backing to match the front. Follow the instructions on page 121 for binding the edges of the quilt. Don't forget to label your quilt.

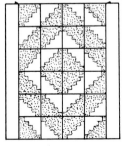

DRUNKARD'S PATH LAP QUILT

A lap quilt is a small quilt, anything from 3½ft (1.07m) to 5ft (1.52m), which can be used in the same way as a travel rug. Children love them, as they become their own piece of home that travels in the car, and from room to room. They can also be used in a student's lodgings, covering a drab bedspread by being placed in a diamond shape on the bed, or even draped on the back of an old sofa.

The thing I like about a lap quilt is that because it is going to be used so much, it just cannot be regarded as an heirloom. So this gives the maker a wonderful sense of freedom to do just what you like – to try new techniques, to try machine quilting, to use all those odd fabrics you have been longing to experiment with. A small quilt does not take too long to make so the person you give it to does not feel intimidated by the responsibility of such a gift.

This lap quilt uses the Drunkard's Path design in two red and two black prints plus a plain red for the corners and borders – simply because I ran out of

I pieced the back of my lap quilt with an original design of strips and cornerstones using scraps of leftover fabric.

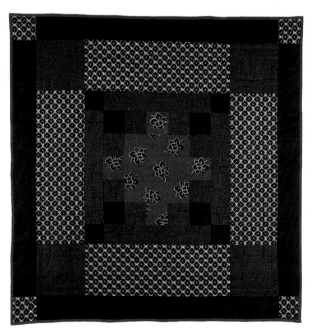

the main fabrics (this is the story of my life!). Three borders have been added because I wanted to use a wonderful African-type dress fabric which I had in my collection. Your lap quilt may not look good with several borders. Try fabric against the basic quilt once it is assembled and make your decision then. The section on adding borders, page 117, should help you with planning a border.

I used all the left-over pieces to make a pieced patchwork reverse side to the quilt (pictured below), with a red and black floral print fabric, which I had been longing to use, in the centre. I only had that one scrap piece, which someone must have given me, so this became the starting point of the pieced back.

FABRIC REQUIREMENTS

18in (45.7cm) each of two red textured and two black fabrics
28in (71.1cm) of plain red fabric for cornerstones and first border plus binding
24in (61cm) fabric for second border
6½ft (2m) of another black fabric for the third border and quilt back
As there will not be enough fabric left in one piece to make the back, enjoy yourself piecing an original design with all your left-over fabric.
Alternatively, find another piece of suitable fabric measuring approximately 56in (142.2cm) square for the back.
Piece of batting 56in (142.2cm) square
Final size of quilt:
54½in (138.4cm) square

CONSTRUCTION

Detailed instructions for cutting out and making up the squares and joining them together are given in the Drunkard's Path, page 49.
1 Make templates from the two curved shapes in Fig 1 page 132, see page 15 for instructions on making templates. They will make a 4in (10.1cm) square, which is 1in (2.5cm) larger than the square

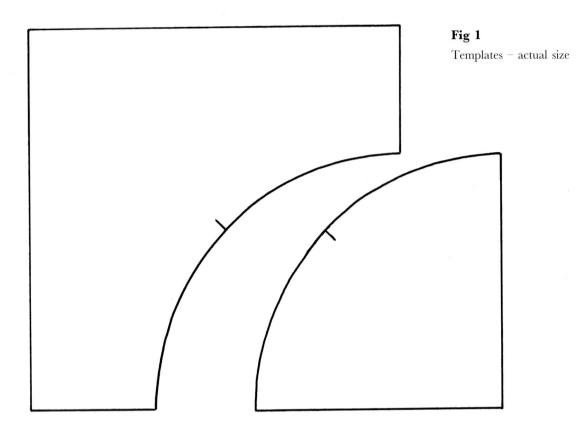

Fig 1
Templates – actual size

used for Drunkard's Path in the sampler quilt block. This is good news as the quilt will grow more quickly and the curves are easier to piece.

2 Study the quilt plan shown in Fig 2 and decide where you will use each of your chosen fabrics. The accompanying key shows how many of each shape you will need in each colour.

3 On the wrong side of the fabric draw around each template the required number of times,

marking the centres. Cut out each shape including the ¼in (6mm) seam allowance.

4 Assemble each of the pieced squares. The various fabric combinations are shown in Fig 3.

5 The design is made in two parts: the main design or central section of pieced squares, plus a frame which combines strips, pieced squares and four corner squares or cornerstones (Fig 4).

The main design comprises sixty-four squares: eight rows each of eight squares (Fig 4). Arrange your squares in this design and machine-stitch them together row by row. Press at each stage from the front of the work.

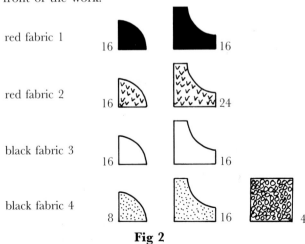

red fabric 1   16   16

red fabric 2   16   24

black fabric 3   16   16

black fabric 4   8   16   4

Fig 2

132

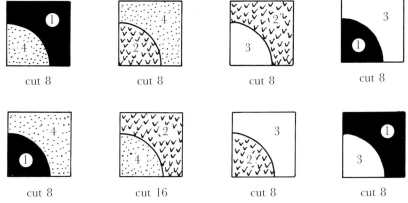

cut 8   cut 8   cut 8   cut 8

Fig 3

cut 8   cut 16   cut 8   cut 8

Fig 4

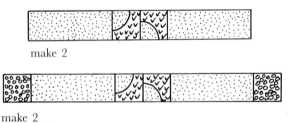

make 2

make 2

Fig 5

6 From the second black fabric cut eight strips each 4½ x 12½in (11.4 x 31.7cm). From the plain red fabric cut four 4½in (11.4cm) squares. Join the strips, squares and remaining pieced squares into two short and two long sets as shown in Fig 5.

7 Pin and machine-stitch the two shorter lengths to opposite sides of the quilt, matching the seams of the pieced squares carefully. Press seams outwards, away from the quilt.

8 Pin and machine-stitch the two longer lengths to the other two sides of the quilt, again matching seams carefully. Press the seams outwards, away from the quilt.

9 For the first border, cut four strips from the plain red fabric each 2 x 40½in (5 x 102.9cm) plus four squares for the cornerstones each 2in (5cm) square. Pin and stitch two strips to either side of the quilt and press seams outwards, away from the quilt. Sew one square to either end of the remaining two strips. Press seams towards the strips (Fig 6). Pin and stitch these to the top and bottom of the quilt, matching the seams carefully.

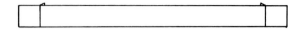

Fig 6

10 For the second border, cut four strips from the chosen fabric, each 2½ x 43½in (6.3 x 110.5cm) and four plain red fabric squares for the cornerstones each 2½ (6.3cm) square. Join the cornerstones and attach the strips to the quilt in the same way as before. Press the strips outwards, away from the quilt.

11 For the third border, cut four strips from the black fabric two each 4 x 47½in (10.1 x 120.7cm) plus four plain red fabric squares for the cornerstones each measuring 4in (10.1cm) square. Join the cornerstones and attach the strips to the quilt in the same way as before. Press the strips outwards, away from the quilt.

12 Either piece a quilt back to your own design or cut a piece of fabric 56in (142.2cm) square, about ¾in (1.9cm) larger than the quilt on all sides. Cut a matching piece of batting.

13 Plan the quilting design and, if necessary, draw it on with a marking pencil before tacking the layers together. For full instructions on quilting see page 110. I quilted this lap quilt by outlining the red shapes at a ¼in (6mm) distance and then just quilting in the seamline of each border strip (Fig 7).

14 When the quilting has been completed, cut and attach the binding strips by following the instructions on page 121.

Fig 7   Quilting design for the lap quilt. All borders are quilted 'in the ditch'.

PROJECT 4

FUN FOR FROGS QUILLOW

A quillow is a small quilt that folds up to fit inside its own cushion. The clever part is that the cushion is attached to the back of the quilt and looks like a matching pocket. The front of the cushion is on the *inside* of this pocket, so that an amazing conjuring trick is performed when the cushion is turned right side out and the quilt folded neatly into it.

Any design can be used for the quilt itself, which measures 3½ x 4½ft (1.07 x 1.31m) and for the cushion which is 18in (45.7cm) square. This quillow uses the machined Rail Fence design for the quilt, while the cushion pocket is made with pieced triangles in a simple propeller block that allows more of the delightful frog fabric to be seen and enjoyed.

FABRIC REQUIREMENTS

28in (71.1cm) of each of three fabrics for the quilt and cushion block
21in (53.4cm) fabric for the border
6½ft (2m) fabric for the quilt back, cushion back and cushion block
Piece of 2oz batting 44 x 54in (112 x 131cm)
Final size of quilt:
42 x 54in (107 x 131cm)
Final size of cushion:
18in (45.7cm) square

CONSTRUCTION

1 Cut twelve strips each 2½in (6.3cm) wide down the length of each of the three fabrics for the Rail Fence design (Fig 1).

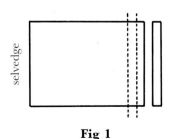

Fig 1

2 Follow the instructions given for Rail Fence, page 27, to stitch the strips into bands, then cut these bands into pieces, each measuring 6½in (16.5cm) square. You need forty-eight squares to make the quilt.
3 Take six of the Rail Fence squares and arrange them in a row as shown in Fig 2. Machine-stitch the row together, using a ¼in (6mm) seam and a small stitch as usual. Press the seams to one side, pressing from the front of the work.
4 Arrange a second row of six squares as shown in Fig 3. Machine-stitch together and press the seams in the opposite direction to those of row one.

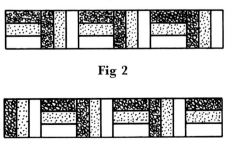

Fig 2

Fig 3

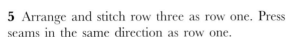

5 Arrange and stitch row three as row one. Press seams in the same direction as row one.

6 Arrange and stitch row four as row two. Press seams in the same direction as row two. Continue in this way until eight rows have been completed.

7 Join the rows together, matching the seams carefully. Press seams to one side from the front.

8 From the border fabric cut four strips each 3¼in (8.3cm) wide. Join them in pairs and press the joining seams open so that they are not noticeable. Measure the length of the quilt down its centre (Fig 4a). Trim either end of each border strip so that the strip matches the measurement with the join exactly in the centre. Pin and stitch these strips to each side of the quilt, easing in any fullness in the quilt to fit the border strips. Press the seams outwards, away from the quilt (Fig 4b).

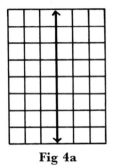

Fig 4a   **Fig 4b**

9 Measure the quilt from side to side across its centre (Fig 4c). From the border fabric cut two strips to match this measurement and 3¼in (8.3cm) wide. Pin and stitch these strips to the top and bottom of the quilt, easing in any fullness (Fig 4d). For more details on adding borders see page 117.

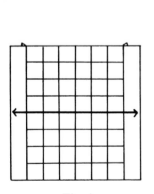

Fig 4c   **Fig 4d**

10 Layer the quilt with batting and backing fabric, cutting both about 1in (2.5cm) larger on all sides. Tack ready for quilting.

11 The quilt was quilted in the seamline (known as 'in the ditch') on the top sides of the frog fabric

strips and also along the top sides of the bubbles fabric strips to accentuate the stepped effect (Fig 5).

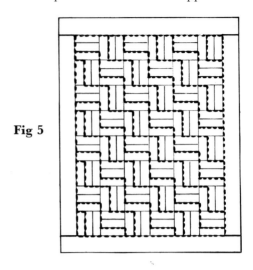

Fig 5

CONSTRUCTING THE POCKET

1 Choose two of the fabrics used in the Rail Fence design. From each cut two 7⅞in (20cm) squares. Cut each square diagonally (Fig 6a).

2 Join each triangle of fabric A to a triangle of fabric B to form four squares (Fig 6b). Press the seams towards the darker fabric.

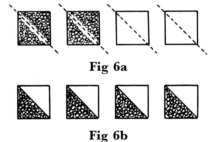

Fig 6a

Fig 6b

3 Arrange these in the propeller block shown in Fig 7. Stitch the top two squares together. Press the seams to one side. Stitch the second two squares together. Press the seams in the opposite direction. Finally stitch the two halves together, matching the centres carefully. Press from the front.

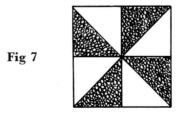

Fig 7

4 Measure the block, it should be 14½in (36.8cm) square. Use 1½in (3.8cm) wide strips of the remaining Rail Fence fabric (Fig 8a) to frame the

block in the same way as the sampler quilt blocks were framed with their sashing strips, see page 110. Repeat this border with 1½in (3.8cm) cut strips of the backing fabric (Fig 8b).

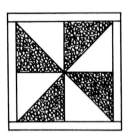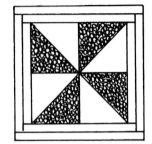

Fig 8a   **Fig 8b**

5 Cut a piece of batting and a piece of backing fabric, using the same fabric as the quilt back, about ½in (1.2cm) larger on all sides than the pieced top.
6 Place the batting on a flat surface and position the backing fabric on it, right side *up*. Place the pieced top right side *down* on to it. Pin and stitch a ¼in (6mm) seam around three sides of the block, leaving the fourth side open (Fig 9).

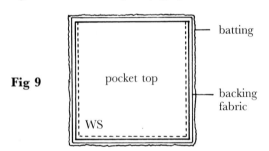

Fig 9   batting

pocket top

WS   backing fabric

7 Trim away the extra batting and backing fabric. Turn the pocket right side out, pushing the corners out carefully without damaging the stitching.
8 Tack the layers together and quilt the block as shown in Fig 10, or feel free to design your own quilting pattern.

ASSEMBLING THE QUILLOW

1 Place the quilt right side *down* on a flat surface and position the pocket centrally at the top end with its right side *down* and the raw edges lined up with the edges of the quilt. Tack these edges together ready for binding (Fig 11).
2 Bind the two sides of the quilt, following the binding instructions on page 121. Next bind the bottom edge and finally the top edges, including the raw edges of both quilt and pocket.
3 Pin and carefully hand-stitch the two sides of the

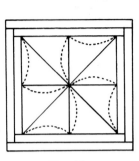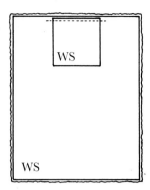

Fig 10   **Fig 11**

cushion in place on the quilt. The bottom side is left open for storing the quilt (Fig 12). The side seams take a lot of strain but must be hand-stitched as any machine-stitching would spoil the front of the quilt. To add strength, stitch into the batting and sew each side twice. Reinforce the corners with extra stitches, and if you can stitch right through without your stitches showing, this will strengthen the corners even more.

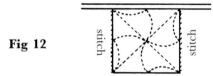

Fig 12   stitch   stitch

FOLDING THE QUILLOW

1 Place the quilt right side *up* on a flat surface. Fold the sides of the quilt over in line with the edges of the pocket (Fig 13a).
2 Pull the pocket through to its right side, enclosing the top two folded sides of the quilt (Fig 13b).
3 Fold the quilt over so that the bottom edges meet the open end of the pocket (Fig 13c).
4 Bring the folded edge up into the pocket so that all the quilt is inside it (Fig 13d).

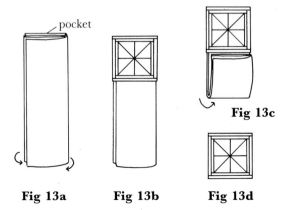

pocket

Fig 13c

Fig 13a   **Fig 13b**   **Fig 13d**

GRANDMOTHER'S FAN QUILT

This quilt for a single bed takes the 12in (30.5cm) Grandmother's Fan block and repeats it to make a curved design that has a similar look to the Drunkard's Path block.

COLOUR CHOICES

The fans are each made from six segments plus a centre. I used a selection of prints, stripes and checks and varied the arrangement in each fan, which gives a random, scrap quilt look to the design. A simpler effect can be obtained by limiting the number of fabrics in each fan to just two or three. The centres need to be stronger in colour than the rest of the fan to give weight.

The background fabric occupies much of the quilt and can look stark if not well quilted. For that reason I chose a white fabric with a tiny blue pattern which softens the large areas.

The first and third borders use an assortment of the fan fabrics to continue the scrap quilt feeling. The middle border is a striped blue fabric very similar in shade to the fabric used for the fan centres. If that fabric had not been available I could easily have used the fan fabric instead.

FABRIC REQUIREMENTS

A total of $6\frac{1}{2}$ft (2m) of medium-weight cotton fabrics for the fan segments

16in (40.7cm) fabric for the fan centres

$6\frac{1}{2}$ft (2m) fabric for the background

51in (1.3m) extra of the fan fabrics for the two pieced borders

51in (1.3m) fabric for the middle border plus the binding

Fabric about $90\frac{1}{2}$ x $66\frac{1}{2}$in (2.3 x 1.69m) for the backing. Cotton sheeting is ideal as it does not need to be joined. If 45in (115cm) wide fabric is used, twice the length of the quilt must be bought 5yd (4.6m). Remove the selvedge edges and join it in three pieces with seams running from top to bottom rather than one

central one. This looks better and makes it less obvious that the fabric has had to be joined from necessity rather than choice (Fig 1).

Piece of batting $90\frac{1}{2}$ x $66\frac{1}{2}$in (2.3 x 1.69m)

Final size of quilt:

$88\frac{1}{2}$ x $64\frac{1}{2}$in (2.25 x 1.64m)

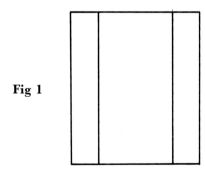

Fig 1

CONSTRUCTION

1 Follow the instructions given in Grandmother's Fan, page 59. Make twenty-four blocks as instructed and trim each one to an exact $12\frac{1}{2}$in (31.7cm) square if necessary.

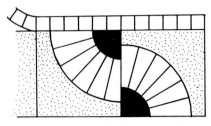

Fig 3

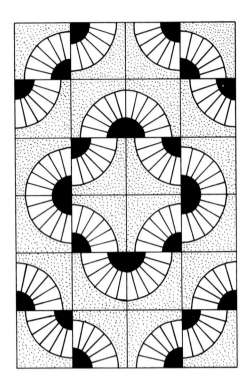

Fig 2

2 Arrange the blocks in the design shown in Fig 2.
3 Machine-stitch together the four blocks in the top row of the quilt with the usual ¼in (6mm) seam. Press the seams to one side from the front of the work. Join the four blocks in the second row. Press the seams in the opposite direction to the top row. Continue to join the blocks into rows until all six rows are complete and the seams pressed alternately to the right and left. If any easing or fudging has to be done to make the fans match in certain parts of the design, remember to always work with the shorter seam on top as this will stretch as you sew.
4 Pin and stitch together rows one and two, matching seams carefully. Continue to pin and stitch each row until the quilt design is complete.
5 Press the seams to one side from the front of the work. If the seams are bulky you may prefer to press the final long seams open from the back of the work.
6 For the first border, cut 124 2½in (6.3cm) squares from the fabrics used in the fan segments. Do this by cutting strips 2½in (6.3cm) wide and then cutting the strips into 2½in (6.3cm) squares, see Trip Around The World, page 36.
7 Join these squares into four lengths, two with thirty-six squares, two with twenty-six squares. Pin and stitch the two longer lengths to each side of the quilt, arranging them so that six squares fit

against each Grandmother's Fan block (Fig 3). Press the squares outwards, away from the quilt.
8 Pin and stitch the remaining two lengths to the top and bottom of the quilt, arranging them so that six squares fit against each block and an extra square is left at either end linking up with the side border squares (Fig 4). Press the border squares outwards, away from the quilt.

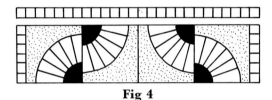

Fig 4

9 The corners of the second border were mitred, but generally it is easier and more appropriate with a series of borders to add sides and then top and bottom, just like sashing.

From the second border fabric cut eight strips each 4½in (11.4cm) wide. Join them in pairs and press the joining seams open so that they are not too noticeable. Measure the length of the quilt down its centre. Trim either end of two of the border strips so that each stip matches this measurement with the join exactly in the centre. Pin and stitch these strips to either side of the quilt, easing in any fullness, see borders page 117. Press the strips outwards, away from the quilt.
10 Measure the quilt from side to side across the centre. Trim either end of the remaining two borders strips so that each strip matches this measurement with the join exactly in the centre. Pin and stitch these strips to the top and bottom of the quilt, easing in any fullness. Press the strips outwards, away from the quilt.
11 For the third border, cut 148 2½in (6.3cm) squares from the fan fabrics as before. Join them into four lengths, two with forty-two squares, two with thirty-two squares. Ideally each longer length will fit exactly on to one side of the quilt, but if this is not the case, avoid trimming down the joined squares as this will look odd. Instead try taking in or letting out the joining seams to give

the exact measurement. It may be fiddly but the end result will look good and you will be glad you took the trouble (you will, really, you will).

12 Pin and machine-stitch the two longer border strips to the sides of the quilt. Press the borders outwards, away from the quilt.

13 Pin and machine-stitch the two shorter strips to the top and bottom of the quilt, adjusting the seams of the joined squares if necessary to match the quilt measurement exactly. Press the borders outwards, away from the quilt.

14 Plan the quilting design and, if necessary draw it on with a marking pencil before tacking the layers together. For full instructions on quilting see page 110. The quilting design used for the fans in this quilt is shown in Fig 5. The background areas were outline quilted ¼in (6mm) away from the edges and then in a 2in (5cm) square grid across

the blocks throughout the background.

15 When all the quilting has been completed, trim the backing and batting to match the front of the quilt and attach binding strips by following the instructions on page 121.

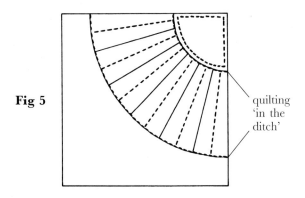

Fig 5

quilting 'in the ditch'

USEFUL ADDRESSES

Associations and Publications
The Quilters' Guild,
OP66 Dean Clough,
Halifax HX3 5AX

National Patchwork Association,
PO Box 300,
Hethersett,
Norwich,
Norfolk NR9 3DB

Patchwork and Quilting Magazine,
Traplet Publications Ltd,
Traplet House,
Severn Drive,
Upton-upon-Severn,
Worcestershire WR8 0JL

Popular Patchwork Magazine,
Nexus Special Interests Ltd,
Nexus House,
Boundary Way,
Hemel Hempstead,
Hertfordshire HP2 7ST

National Quilt Shows
Quilts UK
Organisers:
Elaine Hammond and Dianne
Huck,
Ingsdon,
1 Highfield Close,
Malvern,
Worcestershire WR1 41SH

The National Needlework
Championships
Organisers:
John and Juliet Webster,
National Needlework
Championships,
PO Box 300,
Hethersett,
Norwich,
Norfolk NR9 3DB

The Great British Quilt Festival
Organiser:
Diana Peters,
13 Stourton Road,
Ainsdale,
Southport PR8 3PL

Mail Order Patchwork and Quilting Supplies
The Cotton Patch,
1285 Stratford Road,
Hall Green,
Birmingham B28 9AJ

The Quilt Room,
20 West Street,
Dorking,
Surrey RH4 1BL

Strawberry Fayre,
Chagford,
Devon TQ13 8EN

There are many quilt shops
throughout the country that also
do mail order. Refer to the
patchwork and quilting magazines
for details and advertisements of
specialist shops.

Quilting Events and Activities
Details of current events are listed
in the patchwork and quilting
magazines. Addresses of contacts
for local groups and clubs can
usually be found in the local
library, through the Quilters'
Guild and from specialist quilt
shops in your area.

BIBLIOGRAPHY

Adams, Pauline
Quiltmaking Made Easy
(Little Hills Press, 1990)

Beyer, Jinny
Colour Confidence for Quilters
(Quilt Digest Press, 1994)

Brackman, Barbara
Encyclopedia of Pieced Quilt Patterns
(American Quilters'
Society, 1993)

Chainey, Barbara
The Essential Quilter
(David & Charles, 1993)

Cory, Pepper
Happy Trails
(C & T Publishing, 1991)

Denton and Macey,
Susan and Barbara
Quiltmaking
(Viking O'Neil, 1987)

Hughes, Trudie
Template-free Quiltmaking
(That Patchwork Place, 1986)

Leman and Martin,
Bonnie and Judy
Log Cabin Quilts
(Leman Publications, 1992)

Pellman, Rachel and Kenneth
The World of Amish Quilts
(Good Books, 1984)

Seward, Linda
*The Complete Book of Patchwork,
Quilting and Appliqué*
(Mitchell Beazley, 1987)

Thomas, Donna Lynn
*Shortcuts: A Concise Guide to
Rotary Cutting*
(That Patchwork Place, 1991)

Travis, Dinah
The Sampler Quilt Workbook
(Batsford, 1990)

W I Books
*The Complete Book of Patchwork
and Quilting*
(W I Books Ltd, 1985)

Video: *Sew Simple Patchwork
and Quilting* by Lynne Edwards,
introduced by Una Stubbs
(Workhouse Video, 1992)

ACKNOWLEDGEMENTS

My thanks to the following individuals:

To Jill Carter, whose request for a patchwork class at Coggeshall first made me construct a Sampler Quilt Course.
To Barbara Chainey, who made the link with David & Charles to produce a book based on the course.
To Vivienne Wells, who began the task and to Cheryl Brown who continued it to bring this book into reality.
To Shirley Prescott and Marion Edwards for their expert contributions to the projects.
To the following for allowing their quilts to be used in this book:
Helen Burrett, Pam Croger, Marion Edwards, Sue Fitzgerald, Daphne Green, Jane Hodges, Hazel Hurst, Ann Jones, Kate Kearney, Yvette Long, Ann Larkin, Chris Laudrum, Collie Parker, Shirley Prescott, Sandra Robson, Dot Sidgwick, Jenny Spencer, Shirley Stocks, Mary Telford, Lindy Ward, Chris Wase.

INDEX

Entries in *italic* refer to illustrations